ALL I OWN I OWE

THE AUTOBIOGRAPHY OF REVEREND ALFRED MCBRIDE, O.PRAEM.

ALL I OWN I OWE

THE AUTOBIOGRAPHY OF REVEREND ALFRED MCBRIDE, O.PRAEM.

*"What do you possess that
you have not received?"*

—1 CORINTHIANS 4:7

Cataloging-in-Publication data on file with the Library of Congress.

ISBN: 978-1-61890-399-0

Published in the United States by
Saint Benedict Press, LLC
PO Box 410487
Charlotte, NC 28241
www.SaintBenedictPress.com

Printed and bound in the United States of America.

I dedicate this book to Mrs. Mary Courtney and her brother Michael Corcoran who raised me. I include Catherine Dougherty and her family for being my support throughout my life. I also dedicate this book my Norbertine brothers. I am grateful to Conor Gallagher for inviting me to write this book for Saint Benedict Press.

Contents

CHAPTER ONE

Catholic Life at St. Patrick's

A Launching Pad

The history of a Catholic congregation is not a dry narrative of material achievement. The stateliest temples that men may raise are meaningless save as monuments of faith, of piety and of self sacrifice. This is the purpose of every Catholic parish, to bring forth fruit—fruit that will remain.

—From a sermon delivered on the occasion of the diamond Jubilee of Saint Patrick's Church.

THE Philadelphia of 1839 faced the worst of times. Irish immigrants fled the famine of the old country only to encounter financial panic and the fierce hatred of "Native Americans" (American-born Protestants). The Bill of Rights, which guaranteed religious freedom for all, was ignored when it came to Irish Catholics. However, these immigrants survived their enemies and found jobs bringing to homes the coal shipped to Philadelphia via the Schuylkill River. The diocese decided to establish a parish for these newcomers in what is today Center

City, one block away from the landmark Rittenhouse
Square, a park surrounded by mansions. Today, high-rise
apartments have replaced the great houses. The first St.
Patrick's chapel opened for Mass on December 22, 1839.
A century later I was an altar server among the others
who participated in a series of celebration Masses and
parties that included an Old Timers night on my eleventh birthday.

By the time I came along, the parish included a "new"
church, built in 1910, a Catholic school, fully staffed by
the Sisters of St. Joseph of Chestnut Hill, a convent for the
nine sisters, and a rectory for the four priests. The buildings were located on 20th Street between Locust and
Rittenhouse streets. The parish hall in the school served
as the social center for card parties, Irish dancing, and,
eventually, bingo. Most of the parishioners lived west of
the church. The Upper and Lower Churches each seated
over a thousand people. Sunday Masses were amply
attended, especially during the Second World War. The
eleven o'clock Mass was sung by a men and boy's choir,
the men professional singers either from the Academy of
Music, six blocks away, or the Curtis Institute of Music,
facing Rittenhouse Square.

Four blocks south of the Church is Pine Street which
despite the ebb and flow of demographics has remained
very much the same today as I remember it: a spot for
urban professionals. Mary Courtney (née Corcoran) and
her husband Charles bought a house there at 2022 Pine
in the 1920s. They had one son, Eugene, who served in

World War II, married after the war, but died a few years later after a bout of ill health. After Charles Courtney's early death, Mary's brother, Michael, came to live with her.

On December 12, 1928, I was born and named Alfred after the ill-starred Governor Alfred Emmanuel Smith, the first Catholic to run for president. He was defeated by Herbert Hoover amid yet another surge of anti-Catholicism. I entered the world at the dawn of the Great Depression which was succeeded by World War II. I was baptized in St. Patrick's. My parents were Charles McBride and Mary Shannon, immigrants from Ireland. They did not raise me. I do not remember ever meeting them. I was informally adopted by the widowed Mary Courtney and her bachelor brother Michael. In my early youth I did not pay much attention to this arrangement, even though Mary and Michael were more like grandparents than young parents.

After I began to question the situation, I was told that my birth parents had died. I accepted the explanation but did not receive, nor press for, any details. I had a happy childhood as an adopted only child. Even as I got older I did not have the curiosity that many adopted people have about their family of origin, though I fully understood their interest in learning about their birth parents. I was used to calling Mary "Mom" and never stopped doing so, though I always referred to Michael as Uncle Mike.

Uncle Mike would often take me with him for dinner to his sister Sarah Corcoran's house on Bainbridge

Street. My best memory of those visits was the card game, Euchre, which we played regularly. Once a month on a Sunday, he would take me to his other sister Elizabeth Corcoran's home in West Philadelphia. She lived on Addison Street with her daughter Catherine who was a young adult by the time I met her. Gradually these became my family circle and I treated them as such for that is how they treated me.

The homes in that neighborhood all had porches. Unlike Pine Street where neighborliness was rare, the Addison Street neighbors liked to sit on their porches and enjoy each other's company. Children abounded. Almost all of them were Catholics who belonged to the enormous and stately Transfiguration Church. I was told the parish school had a thousand children.

Hillary Clinton was fond of saying, "It takes a village to raise a child." It makes me think of Addison Street teeming with parents and children where all the parents shared in supervising and caring for all the kids. I loved my visits to "aunts" Lizzie and Catherine. I relished the rich supply of kids to play with. Sadly, after the War, black emigration, blockbusting, and white flight changed the demographics. That parish collapsed and the palatial church has been torn down.

On Pine Street, we were poor in a neighborhood whose residents appeared far better off than ourselves. But we had enough to eat, in a warm house in a beautiful location. Our three-storey house had a small living room, dining room, and kitchen on the first floor. There were two bedrooms on each of the other floors and just one bathroom. The cellar had a coal-fed furnace. Our income was modest at best, but food was inexpensive. Still, we needed the monthly food check that the parish St. Vincent de Paul Society deposited at McGonagle's store for us. Living close to the business and shopping district meant one could easily walk to the fascinating center of the city.

On our block there was only one other Catholic family, the Dougherty's, and their children were grown. As far as I could tell, there were no Catholic children close by. There were black kids who lived on the next street south of us. I made friends and played with them. But when I was eight, they shied away from me, telling me that I was not welcome any more. I was disappointed and went to one of the parents who told me it was time to separate. I reported this at home only to find they agreed. Despite the sentiments of my elders, I did not acquire a prejudice against black folks. A year later, I was playing in Rittenhouse Square with a boy that had a tricycle. He let me ride on the back. He decided to race the bike which hit a stone and turned over. After my fall I could not stand up without pain. My leg was broken. The boy ran away, and I sat on the ground and cried as people passed by. After a while a black man stopped, picked me up, and carried me home. Since we had no car, Uncle Mike carried me to Children's Hospital where I spent a full week in bed with sandbags and wooden splints keeping my leg in place before they put a cast on it.

When I returned home my rescuer stopped by several times to see how I was doing. I have never forgotten his kindness. After I returned to school, the sisters instructed Bobby Lynch to walk me home for the next three weeks until they judged I no longer needed help.

* * *   * * *   * * *

In fifth grade I began taking piano lessons for twenty-five cents a lesson from the sister who taught music. We had a good piano at home so it was convenient to practice. I learned to read sheet music, and three years later, the new music teacher offered to teach me how to play the organ, free of charge. The transition from piano to organ was relatively simple once the new touch was mastered. By the middle of my eighth-grade year, I volunteered to play the organ for most of the evening services at the church: sodality on Thursday night; First Fridays for Sacred Heart devotions; nine-day novenas for the celebration of St. Francis Xavier's feast; and the week-long missions for men and women.

Two girls, Mary Gorman and Henrietta Moccia, were also trained to play the organ which relieved me from a number of obligations.

Although my organ playing was volunteer work, I did earn a little cash for cleaning the leftover wax out of the vigil lights. Once in a while I dusted the pews in the Upper Church. I also took care of the pamphlet racks that were stationed at each entry to the Lower Church, deciding which authors to carry and making the orders. My standard was simple: I noted which ones sold the most copies. The winner was Jesuit Daniel Lord. Pamphlets from the Redemptorists were popular as well. I guess I also was swayed by the look of the covers.

I also served Mass at the parish. You may think I scarcely left church, but I had many other interests. These little duties made me familiar with the workings of the church and I felt at home around the altar, the organ, and the devotional shrines of the Lower Church.

Still, my life in the outside world was robust. Since the parish school had a relatively small area to play in, during their breaks from class, I got to know the students who gathered after school on Rittenhouse Street right next to St. Patrick's.

The gathering place was the home of the Moccia family. Mom and Pop Moccia came from Italy, she from Naples and he from a town east of Naples. When they came to America the two of them happened to wind up on the same street in the Italian district in South Philadelphia. They fell in love, married, and eventually wound up on Rittenhouse Street. Mr. Moccia obtained a job as a chauffeur for Mr. Harrison who lived in a high-rise apartment building on Locust Street just one block away.

Mr. Harrison also expected Mr. Moccia to check on the care of the car's engines, tires, and other mechanicals. Mr. Harrison owned a house on Rittenhouse Street that had a garage on the first floor and a spacious apartment on the second and third floors. Mr. Moccia was compensated for driving the car and caring for it with a salary and the use of the apartment. Mr. and Mrs. Moccia had four children: Girard, Bob, Henrietta, and Angelina.

In the summer time, "Mama" Moccia brought her folding chairs outside the garage and welcomed her children's friends to sit down and get to know her and her family. I took full advantage of her welcoming friendliness.

Bob became my best friend and remains so to this day. I have been able to celebrate Thanksgiving with him, his wife Ria, and their extended family for the past twenty years. In those days, Bob and I would cut a tennis ball in half and, using a broomstick, bat it against the façade of building for scores, or we would create chalk bases in the street and use a tennis ball and the broomstick as a bat. On hot days we ran out to the Philadelphia Art Museum and jumped and splashed in the fountains until guards chased us away. We had a grand time. Things got even better when a Polish family, the Senskes, moved to Rittenhouse Street, adding three more guys to our group.

* * *   * * *   * * *

In eighth grade, I met the best teacher of my years at St. Patrick's school, Sister Bartholomew Marie. She was tall and well-prepared. In our first class she said, "I plan to give you what you need to be accepted in a Catholic high school." In those days, 1941, very few of us had our eyes on college. Sister Bart, as we called her, was a wonder, involving us in a variety of ways throughout each class day. On a typical morning, several of us wrote an assignment on the blackboards, while others wrote or read at their desks. Meanwhile, three or four stood ready to answer questions she would pose. Slow readers worked at reading machines that covered pages at faster paces to quicken the reader's capacity. This might be followed by a typical class project and then we rotated to different exercises as before.

One thing I recall with special gratitude occurred after lunch and fresh air in the school yard. Sister Bart distributed a slim booklet filled with one-line prayers. Together we recited three or four pages each afternoon. Some quotes were from scripture and others were devotional prayers such as: "Jesus, meek and humble of heart, make our hearts like unto yours" . . . "O Mary, conceived without sin, pray for us who have recourse to you" . . . "My Jesus , Mercy" . . . "I love you Lord, and I lift my voice to worship you" . . . "May we give glory to your name, Lord" . . . "We adore you O Lord and we praise you. For by your holy cross you have redeemed the world." We recited these so often that many of us never forgot them, and the little prayers would bubble to our lips in times of trouble and anxiety. Only in later life would I read St. Augustine's comment on the value of a prayer custom among Egyptian monks who used short prayers like darts sent forth to God.

One day in the second semester Sister Bart asked me to stay after class. I wondered if I had done something wrong, but she wanted to prepare me to enter the Spelling Bee, and to compete for a scholarship to the prestigious Jesuit high school at the corner of 18th Street and Stiles.

I was honored and did my best to respond to the drills after school. I began to realize that she added this burden to her teaching day when she might have relaxed after classes ended.

On the day of the competition, a Sunday afternoon, I joined the other students. Slowly, I made my way through the competition and was one of the last two boys remaining. I was given the word, "sagacity." I said, "S-A-G-A-S-I-T-Y." *Bong!* The bell tolled for my defeat. I was awarded a half scholarship, but I could not accept it because I did not have the money, nor did Mom or Uncle Mike, to cover the other half. I returned to the convent that afternoon and gave the news to Sister Bart who probably was in the chapel praying for my success. She was calm and positive in her reply: "Well, Alfred, you gave it your best. Now we move on to assuring your future education."

Some twenty years later, I was giving a lecture in a big hall filled with Catholic school teachers, many of them nuns, of the Newark diocese. In my speech I referred to the latest trend in education—Individually Guided Instruction. Instead of explaining the theory, I described my experience as a student under Sister Bartholomew Marie. I told them how she taught, and explained that *that* was what Individually Guided Instruction was. At the close of the day, as I was leaving the auditorium, several nuns ran up to me shouting, "She's here! She's here!" Sure enough, right behind them was Sister Bart, tall and dignified as ever, feelings under control. Suddenly my inner little boy appeared and she seemed once again to be that mighty presence before me. I was thrilled that I had been able to praise her before a large audience and to discover she was there. It was a small gift to her for the tremendous gifts she gave me in her education of my life.

Three years later, her sister sent me a note that Sister Bart was celebrating her golden jubilee as a nun. She was teaching at Catholic school in New Jersey, and she did not want any guests other than her relatives and the school children but would welcome prayers. I sent her a letter along with my commentary on the Acts of the Apostles, *The Gospel of the Holy Spirit*. Her thank you letter expressed her deep feelings of gratitude along with this touching request: "Father, I hope and pray that if it is possible, you will be the celebrant of the Mass of the Resurrection at my funeral." I replied that I would love to do that and promised I would honor her wishes. At the same time, I wondered where I would be or whether I would be free.

God took care of those details. He brought her home on the feast of St. Bartholomew, August 24, just as I was completing a retreat for our community at St. Norbert Abbey. I arrived at Chestnut Hill in plenty of time. She was laid out in an open casket in front of the altar. I whispered to her that, at long last, I can spell sagacity because of her impact on my life. "Rest in peace, dear heart."

* * *   * * *   * * *

Another important event occurred during my last semester in the eighth grade. One early spring Saturday afternoon, I went to confession to Father Graham. After I had confessed my sins and received my penance, Fr. Graham said, "Alfred you have the 7:00 a.m. Mass next week," meaning that was my server's assignment. "Also, go across the street to Mrs. Harvey's employment agency. She has a job for you."

"Thank you, Father."

Within the hour I went to Mrs. Harvey's and received my first major, regular paying job. She told me about a couple who had a suite in the Warwick hotel, just a block beyond Rittenhouse Square. They wanted me to walk their dog three times a day for five dollars a week. I loved dogs and had always walked a lot, so it was a perfect fit.

Mrs. Harvey advised, "Shine your shoes, put on clean clothes and scrub your finger nails." Such preparations completed, I went to the servants' entrance and took their elevator to the tenth floor. As soon as I entered, Skipper, a lively Irish Terrier, jumped all over me and I felt right at home. My employers were Captain Taylor Smith, head of Naval Intelligence in Philadelphia, and his wife Ellen Wallace Smith. From privileged families, they grew up in Fredericksburg, Virginia, and there married. They had just arrived from a tour of duty in Berlin where Taylor served as the American naval attaché to the Hitler regime. A typical intelligence officer, he never spoke about his work. Mrs. Smith, however, did reveal stories about their social life in Berlin, often diplomatic parties where Hitler and his chief Nazi officials were present.

I began reading the war stories in the newspapers and

looked for comments from them which gave Mrs. Smith an opportunity to talk more about life in Berlin before the war. One point she often stressed was the persecution of the Jews. The house they had lived in had been taken from a Jewish family by the government and the family had been sent to a death camp. Moreover, the state appointed the servants who served as spies in their home.

One of the perks of working in the Warwick Hotel was access to the servant's elevator. There was always the leftover food—steaks, desserts, and other goodies— which supplemented my teen appetite. That all changed when, several months later, the Smiths moved one block away to a two bedroom apartment. Their daughter, Lucy Decker, was married to a submarine commander whose ship patrolled the east coast to spot German ships trying to deposit spies ashore, or other subs set on sinking American ships. His sub anchored each month at Groton, Connecticut. Lucy decided to take an apartment there to meet her husband when he came into port. Their young boys, Randy and Joel Porter (addressed as JP) came to live with their grandparents. I was enlisted to get them enrolled in St. Patrick's school and often served as their sitter when the grandparents went out to dinner. This— as well as washing Skipper on Saturdays—added fees to my salary.

CHAPTER TWO

High School with the Norbertines

THE next big development in my life was high school. I enrolled at Southeast Catholic High School. Situated at 9th and Christian Streets in the colorful Italian market district, it was fourteen city blocks away from my home. This made for a busy morning. I rose early and stopped at a bakery to fortify myself with a large cinnamon roll. This was followed by a seven-block walk to get Skipper and a twenty minute walk with him. Then I would catch a trolley to 9th Street and complete the trip to school with another seven-block walk.

In 1942 most of the teachers at Southeast Catholic were Norbertines. They wore white habits. Two-thirds were priests. The rest were seminarians who took theology classes either before or after teaching their five daily classes. The majority were strict, no-nonsense teachers, mostly from Wisconsin while the seminarians were mainly Philadelphians.

I was used to firm nuns, so becoming accustomed to firm males was no adjustment other than their being tough physical punishers if needed. A small detail won me over. Their handwriting on the board was as abysmal as mine, a testimony to my inability ever to master the Palmer Method of writing. I was accustomed to the priests at St. Patrick's, but they remained distant. There was no sense of a relationship with them other than a formal one. Father Dolan who taught at Thomas More High School was the exception. In the sacristy while vesting for Mass, he would briefly chat with us, but that was it. The Norbertines outside the classroom were generally friendly and outgoing, which was different than what I was accustomed to. Despite, the friendliness of the Norbertines, I simply did not have much time to have a relationship any of them. I rushed in at morning class time and rushed out at the close of the day to get on with Skipper and other duties.

I did not sign up for any outside activities because I had no time for them. Besides, I was too short to play basketball and too small to play football. I did, however, attend virtually all the games. In my junior year, our school won the Catholic League basketball championship. We were to play Southern Public High School for the city championship at Convention Hall on a Thursday night. I was booked to play the organ that night for the sodality. I asked Mary Gorman and Henrietta Moccia to take my place. They both refused being otherwise engaged. When Thursday arrived, angry and frustrated, I did my duty, raced out of church to the Walnut Street trolley to get to Convention Hall. I ran to the ticket office and was denied entrance. Twelve thousand fans packed the hall and no others were allowed in.

Suddenly, I noticed a bunch of boys running to the

back of the building. I found myself running with them, climbing through open basement windows, dashing through dark corridors, up the stairs, and, suddenly, in basketball heaven, sitting on the steps with less than a minute to go. Southern was one point ahead. Joe Gorman and "Toad" Hannan (both parishioners at St. Patrick's) took control of the ball and moved it quickly up the court, zipped it to Larry Faust, our star center, who sank it through the net to the elation of the six thousand South Catholic High fans. Joe Gorman and I still see each other regularly around Thanksgiving and shamelessly re-live that moment, much as I am doing here.

By the end of my junior year, the war in Europe had ended. Captain Smith retired from office and he and his wife were returning to their home in Annapolis. It would be goodbye to Skipper. But, to my surprise they invited me to spend the summer in their home. I received permission from home and moved to Annapolis for the summer. Their home was called Acton House named after the colonial builder of the property. It was a typical, red brick, colonial-style home. There was a large front lawn and an even bigger one in back that bordered the Severn River from which I could see the Naval Academy in the distance. It would my last time with them and Skipper.

The Smiths introduced me to Jimmy Meredith who lived next door. He was my age and had a row boat in which we navigated the river. He taught me how chop eels, put a chunk on a fishing line, and catch an endless line of crabs, which I would bring up to the cook for our meals.

I went to Mass at St. Mary's, a Redemptorist church. I was saddened to see that black parishioners had to sit in the back pews and go to Communion last. Apart from this unfortunate experience, I had a terrific summer that was capped by the end of the Japanese war. I joined the throngs on the main street. Then the next week I bade farewell to the Captain and Ellen. I owed them a lot more than a salary. They gave me confidence in life and a glimpse of other opportunities out there. I also thanked Jimmy for his friendship and wished him well. I would never see Captain Smith or Jimmy again, but, after my ordination eight years later, I visited Mrs. Smith two more times before her death.

* * *   * * *   * * *

At an early age, I developed a love for movies. On Saturday afternoons I would go to the Avon Movie on South Street. For a tiny fee I could see Movietone News, followed by what were called "chapters," twenty-minute segments of a long story that always ended with the hero or heroine in life or death struggles such as a knife headed for the heart. We had to wait 'till next week to find out what happened. After this I could sit back and watch a double header, two movies that rounded out the afternoon. In my high school years my attention turned to the first run shows downtown.

One of my favorite movies was *The Song of Bernadette*. My attraction to the film can be traced back to the Lower Church in St. Patrick's which had what we now call the "devotional setting." There was a Lourdes shrine and stat-ues of saints arranged all along the walls on each side, with flickering vigil candles casting a warm glow throughout the Lower Church. The shrine and the statues and the candles are all there to this day. I was especially attracted to the Lourdes shrine, a devotion to Bernadette's vision of the Blessed Mother.

The film recounted Bernadette's visions of Our Lady and the doubts she faced from her family, friends, and the local pastor. Finally, the pastor told her, "Get the lady's name!"

In her final vision, Bernadette asked the lady her name and the lady responded, "I am the Immaculate Conception." Bernadette barely knew her catechism and did not know the meaning of this name. When she told the pastor, he was amazed for he knew she could not have made this up. It was undeniable now: she was seeing Mary the Mother of Jesus, conceived without sin. In the lobby afterwards I was surprised to hear someone say, "It was a touching film. Of course I don't believe a word of it." I was tempted to remind that person of the caution at the start of the story, "To those who believe, no explanation is necessary. To those who do not believe, no explanation will suffice. Only faith understands this truth."

Another of my favorites was a film called *Mrs. Miniver*, an inspiring and thrilling tale of the patriotism of the British people. It told the story of the rescuing of thousands of their troops trapped near the beaches of Dunkirk in Normandy. My custom at the time was to by a little box of chocolate covered caramels which I would munch during the film. So absorbed was I by this story and so heated was my system that the candy melted in my pocket. I was deeply embarrassed and did what I could to conceal it.

I also recall seeing the acclaimed film, *Going My Way*, in which Bing Crosby played a singing priest and Barry Fitzgerald played a crabby Irish priest. The story was set in an inner-city parish with lots of financial problems. It was an extraordinary hit followed by *Bells of St. Mary's* headlined by Ingrid Bergman who looked stunning as a nun with Crosby replaying his singing priest role.

Movies, at that time, were a wholesome, often uplifting, escape, but the post-war societal changes did away with such innocent and idealistic plots. No more fairy tales. We went headlong into realism, despair, absurdity, sex, and violence. Fortunately, God led me out of the theaters and into the Norbertine Order. There, for the next eight years, I was well-shielded from what the "world" was doing to itself.

What attracted me to the Norbertines?

My arrival at Southeast Catholic High School was just what I needed for my teen years. I entered an all-male environment with 1,200 boys and forty Norbertines as my teachers. I could not ask for a better environment to cope with my physical, psychological, and moral growing pains. Though my main contact with them was in the classroom because I was so occupied with my various jobs, those four years with the Norbertines gave me what I needed for the process of maturity.

I rarely had personal contact with individual teachers, with the major exception of Bob Cornell. With him, it was exclusively as a student in a classroom, but that was enough for me to have a personal admiration for how he taught and for the passion for his subject that he shared.

I admired the teachers who could control the classes with very little overt effort. Usually they were men who were well prepared, faithful to following up on their demands, and fair in their treatment of students, in testing, giving marks, and evaluations. They expertly linked religion to a variety of topics. Despite my relationships with the Norbertines being limited to the classroom, I developed a special admiration for certain teachers that played a large role in my finally applying to the Order. The tipping point was a direct invitation by Father Victor de Cleene, as I will describe in a moment.

My sophomore year marked the beginning of my friendship with Frater Bob Cornell (Frater is Latin for brother, a title applied to Norbertine seminarians). I was assigned to his home room, where we met for fifteen minutes at the start of the school day. Usually, we heard messages over the sound system and then discussed any issues that needed attention. Cornell was all business and meetings with him were very brief. In my junior year I took his course on American history. He was brilliant. An orderly lecturer he rarely seemed to consult notes as

he took us on the wild ride of colonial times, the revolution, the constitution, and the liberation from England.
We learned about Washington and the American
revolution, Lincoln and the Civil war, the aftermath, and
then proceeded into modern times. He peppered us with
constant quizzes, which he always corrected overnight,
and tests, which he also corrected in a timely manner. We
were never in the dark about his expectations. His classroom was immaculate. In the last week he told us he was
being ordained to the priesthood at the Norbertine school
chapel of Archmere Academy in Claymont, Delaware. He
invited us to come. I attended the ceremony and received
his first blessing.

As a senior I signed up for another Cornell course,
"National Problems." This course was close to his heart
because he was a strong supporter of the papal encycli-
cals on social justice and a dyed-in-the-wool supporter of
the Democratic Party which he argued best fulfilled the
Church's social teachings. In a few years he would complete a doctoral degree in American history and write a
thesis on the Anthracite Coal Strike, a turning point for
the emerging power of the unions. He returned to De
Pere, Wisconsin, as a professor at St. Norbert College and
became an active member of the Wisconsin Democratic
Party. I will pick up that story a little later in this book.

Another teacher who had an impact on me was Father
Rentmeester. Since math was one of my weaker subjects
I relied on Father Rentmeester to help me to understand
the mysteries of advanced algebra. His teaching method

was just right for me. Our textbook contained a series of lessons that were augmented by exercises in the rear of the book. Father would take about thirty minutes to explain the lesson and then assign an exercise for homework which we began working on in class. While we did that he went around to each of us (about thirty-five students). When he came to me he would always say, "How are you doing? Do you have any difficulty with today's lesson?" His personal interest impressed me and much to my surprise I did know the subject, eventually earning an A.

Another priest who influenced me in those years was Father Van Dyke, my Latin teacher. Not by personal choice, I was scheduled by the Norbertine registrar to take four years of Latin. I was among those who scored in the A level, all of whom were required to take the first two years of Latin. I was used to Latin, having been an altar server at St. Patrick's. But now I began to learn grammar, vocabulary, conjugations, and declensions. In the third year, I found Cicero a bit mysterious and not too relevant. But I woke up in senior year with Virgil. I'm glad I did because years later with pleasure I taught Virgil to seniors at St. Norbert High School next to our Abbey.

By junior year the number of Latin students diminished to about fifteen boys. It did not take me long to figure out that the registrar selected us for advanced Latin because we were thought to have a possible vocation to the priesthood. We spoke about it openly with each other. The planners were right; eleven of us went on to become priests. Four of us became Norbertines, six joined the archdiocese, and one joined the Franciscans. Father Van Dyke was the right teacher for these courses. He was cheerful, demanding, and tireless. It was less like a classroom and more like a seminar or even a tutorial.

Several of my classmates in the Latin courses volunteered to serve private Masses at the Norbertine faculty house. In those days there was no concelebration. Each priest would offer a private Mass each day unless he was assigned to an early Mass in neighboring parishes. I was never free to do this. But the ones who could were invited to a more personal spiritual contact with Norbertines than was possible for me

As the end of my high school days approached, I began to wonder what was next. I had thought of priesthood but spoke about it to no one. Then, one day, I received a message that Father Victor De Cleene, the school principal, wanted to see me. I had the usual reaction of a student mysteriously summoned to the principal's office and scanned my behavior to see what I might have done wrong that had come to his attention. I need not have worried. He said to me, "Alfred, we believe you have a vocation to the priesthood. If you wish to be a diocesan priest, we will help you get into St. Charles Seminary. If you would like to be a Norbertine, we would love to have you and would welcome you." I felt awkward, yet, somewhere inside, pleased. I was at a loss for words, managing only to say, "Thank you, Father," before walking out somewhat dazed.

My teachers and their influence on me through thousands of hours in Norbertine classrooms constituted remote preparation for joining the Order. The proximate event supplied by Father De Cleene sealed the deal. I went to Father Cornell and Father Joe Dorff (I took his chemistry class) and asked them what they thought. They encouraged me to apply to the community and told me how to go about it. They were open to any questions I had. At home I discussed the possibility with Mom and Uncle Mike. I need not have been surprised by their ready approval; being strong Irish Catholics, they cherished the priesthood. I took a while before sharing the news with the Rittenhouse Square "gang." I was a bit shy about it. They said little and did not seem surprised. In many ways, as I learned in life, others often know more about you than you do of yourself.

The details for moving to Wisconsin were fairly simple. In early June 1946, we were expected to board a train at the B&O (Baltimore and Ohio) train station bound for Chicago where we changed trains for Green Bay. I put on my newly purchased black suit and shoes, white shirt, and black tie. I packed my scarce belongings in a scruffy old suitcase and took a trolley to the station. I knew three of my classmates from our third and fourth year Latin classes—Vince Conway, John Cox, and Bob Kelly—and was introduced to Henry Jafolla from the class of '45.

Just before we left, Father Cornell appeared to wish us a safe trip and a good arrival in De Pere. In retrospect this may seem to some today to be too swift a process

between the end of high school in Philadelphia and seminary in Wisconsin. I guess that those were simpler times
and my whole Catholic upbringing fostered at home and
strengthened by twelve years of strong Catholic schools
and outstanding Christian witness by nuns and priests
produced an inevitability that made the transition seem
perfect.

It might be said that I laid the city boy to rest as I
entered the rural, Midwest world of St. Norbert Abbey,
what was then a rural culture. St. Norbert College was
on the Abbey campus and was run by the Holland-born
Abbot Pennings, who also oversaw four high schools, one
each in De Pere, Green Bay, Philadelphia, and Claymont,
Delaware. He also presided over twenty-five parishes
staffed by Norbertines. I would soon find out that the
community had a strong pastoral spirit witnessed by the
Abbot, a respect for the ministry of education and a broad
variety of talents placed at the service of the Church and
its people.

I brought with me the faith-based culture of a small
Irish family. I owe a lifetime of gratitude to Mom and
Uncle Mike, along with Aunt Lizzie, Aunt Catherine, and
Aunt Sarah for watching over me through my childhood
and teen years. My love for them will never die. I also
brought the impact of St. Patrick's, an identity shaped
through the school, the altar, and the devotional warmth
I savored, providing the music that devout Catholics
loved to sing. I also owed a great deal to the Norbertine
teachers who widened my horizons, helped me grow up,

and planted the self-discipline I would need for the adult life lying before me. I benefited from my pals who served as the brothers whom I lacked and taught me how to have a sense of humor. My four years with Skipper whom I felt was "my" dog and Captain Smith and his wife opened me to people of education, wealth, and heritage. They were my first encounter with Protestants (Episcopalians) and their humanity and goodness sowed in me what future ecumenism would validate.

Among my departing memories, I should mention the corner drug store on Pine Street where I came to know its owners. Their names escape me, but not their natural parental influence on me. They were an elderly Jewish couple from Poland who, thank God, escaped before the Nazi holocaust could destroy them. They liked to teach me lessons. When I once tendered a twenty dollar bill to pay for an inexpensive item, they said, "Put this back in your pocket and pay with your change. Once you break this bill you will spend it quickly." When I began to earn extra cash, I occasionally stopped there after the Sunday Mass and for forty cents ordered bacon and eggs, a feast! They were proud of their Polish heritage and often compared it with Russia which they felt lacked what Poland offered them. Little did I imagine then I would one day write my doctoral dissertation on a Polish-born Rabbi, Abraham Joshua Heschel.

The Sisters of St. Joseph over eight years formed us in the faith and made sure we knew the Catechism and how to live its teachings. They expected us to attend Sunday

Mass and questioned us about it on Monday. They taught us to memorize the Apostles' Creed, the Our Father, Hail Mary, Glory Be, and the Act of Contrition. They pushed frequent Communion, Confession, clean, moral living, and trust in God's mercy. They educated us in reading, writing, arithmetic, history, geography, and spelling. God love you Sisters!

As I look back at these foundational years of my life, I gratefully marvel at the providence of God which so wondrously surrounded me. God's providence provided me with family and friends, a good education, and, above all, a deep, experiential, living Catholic faith mediated through various parish involvements and the influential example of the dedicated sacrifice of religious men and women. The various environments reinforced in me a clear set of values and principles that have directed and enriched my entire life.

CHAPTER THREE

Religious Life in Wisconsin
A Window on Tradition

OUR train left Chicago and brought us directly to De Pere. The name of the town in English means "of the father." It may be traced to a mission station established by Jesuit missionary Father Marquette on this spot in 1673. Originally it was called the Rapids of the Fathers Mission. A Norbertine seminarian met us and drove us the short distance to a house, called the Villa, across the street from the Abbey. John McLaughlin, a candidate from the Norbertine Archmere Academy, was there to meet us. The Fox River bordered our new home where we would live for the summer. Father Peter Wagner was house master for the summer. Now a gentle, elderly man, he was formerly known as "Black Pete" due to his stern presence during his years teaching and monitoring the boarding students at St. Norbert High School in Boyle Hall on campus.

We were introduced to the founding Abbot, Bernard Pennings, O. Praem., then in his eighties. He looked happy to see us, asked a few questions, and blessed us. Our schedule for the summer included classes in Boyle

Hall on topics such as the Life of St. Norbert and the history of the Order and the Abbey. We attended Mass in St. Joseph's Church which, in addition to being a parish church, served the Abbey for major celebrations such as vestitions, making simple and solemn vows, and ordination to the priesthood.

We discovered that three hundred nuns were obtaining their bachelor degrees over a series of twenty summers in St. Norbert's summer school. They presented a colorful parade of diverse habits and devotional customs. They were cheerful and welcoming to us as our paths often crossed. Many of the summer school professors were nuns with degrees in a broad spectrum of liberal arts topics. We ate our meals in the Knight Club which was housed in a new dorm called Residence Hall then, but now is named "Burke Hall" after a Norbertine who devoted much of his life to fund raising for the college. He earned a doctorate in Canon Law at Rome's Gregorian University. The time passed quickly and pleasantly.

We were called postulants, that is, candidates seeking membership in the Norbertines. One midsummer evening, our buddy, Tony, a Wisconsin native, suggested we get a beer at one of the numerous bars on Main Street and we agreed. Not too long after we had downed the first beer, we were approached by a plainclothes officer of the state government supervisors of bars who questioned our ages. I and two others were age seventeen in a place where the age limit was eighteen. We had to leave and he would report this to Father Wagner. The community probably paid fines. Sheepishly, we met with our house master the next morning where we were rebuked, warned, and reminded that our evaluations would contain this event. Despite this incident, in mid-August we were told that the Philadelphians were accepted by the Abbot. Alas, Tony was not. But he did go on to be a diocesan priest for Green bay and served with honor until he died. We made a silent eight-day retreat prior to reception in the community. We were surprised by a new candidate who made the retreat with us. This was Louis Vande Castle, a veteran officer from World War II, an alumnus of the college, and a De Pere native. Being vested in the Norbertine white habit took place on the feast of St. Augustine on August 28.

The habit consists of a robe, a scapular which is placed over the robe and covers its front and back. A short cape bearing a miniature hood is put on next. Lastly, a sash binds the robe and scapular. The ceremony took place at a solemn high Mass in the Abbey church. Those making simple and solemn vows were also a major part of the service. While the church was filled, none of our Philadelphia relatives were present due to the distance and cost.

Our ceremony was simple. After the sermon we lined up before Abbot Pennings. He said, "Dear Sons, what do you ask from us?" We replied, "The mercy of God and the companionship of this Church." The Abbot then said, "May the One who has begun the good work in you bring it to fulfillment before the day of Christ Jesus." We were given our habits and retired to put them on. Today in our reformed rites, the vesting does not take place at Mass. Meanwhile the more elaborate rites for those taking vows continues. When Mass was resumed, we appeared in the sanctuary for the rest of the Eucharist. A celebratory dinner followed and we ate our first meal with the community. We spent time with the second year novices and those in vows. The following morning we drove to Madison where we spent our first year novitiate. We were on our way to an adventure to be trained in the ideals of St. Norbert and the history and traditions of an community nearly a thousand years old.

The Story of St. Norbert

> Father, you made bishop Norbert an outstanding minister of your Church, renowned for his preaching and pastoral zeal. Always grant to your Church faithful shepherds to lead your people to eternal salvation
> —Liturgy of St. Norbert, June 6

Permit me to share with you a few key historical details of St. Norbert's life and mission along with my meditations on his gifts to us. Norbert's dream has endured from the Middle Ages to modern times. His ideals have inspired his vision of religious life through many twists and turns of history so that today his Order is found on all continents. This is the house that Norbert built with the grace of God, the intercession of Mary, and the dedication of countless members. During our novitiate we would be introduced to St. Norbert. It is the story of our community.

Norbert was born in 1080 in the town of Xanten in north Germany not far from the border with Holland. The name of the town derives from Roman times when it was a military camp. The Roman occupiers martyred a number of local, faithful Christians, and so it was called Xanten, meaning Saints.

Norbert's noble family lived in a castle not far from town. According to medieval custom, as the third son, he was destined to dedicate his life to the Church. Norbert was ordained a subdeacon and served with the local cathedral canons. He was not enthusiastic about his vocation, however, and embarked on a life of pleasure unbefitting of his calling. One day, as he was on his way to a party, an electric storm knocked him from his horse and filled him with fear for his life. When he recovered he determined to pursue real Christianity. He went to the Benedictine Abbey of Siegburg where he lived a life of penance and prayer.

He let go of his wealth, presented himself to the Bishop of Cologne Cathedral for ordination to the priesthood, and entered the service of the Emperor Henry V as a chaplain. Accompanying the Emperor on a trip to Rome, he underwent another religious conversion, this time becoming a missionary to France. Pope Gelasius II named him an apostolic preacher, an honor that was repeated by his successor, Calixtus II.

In France, St. Norbert preached, negotiated peace among warlords, and settled family quarrels. He witnessed fidelity to celibacy for priests who had abandoned their vow of chastity. His also focused on the renewal of faith in the Real Presence of Christ in the Eucharist. Tragically, in those times, a priest named Berengar of Tours preached that Jesus was only symbolically present in the consecrated bread and wine. Berengar confused clergy and laity alike and spread the virus of disbelief all too successfully. Norbert countered with Christ's teachings on the Eucharist, especially as found in the "Bread of Life" lessons in the sixth chapter of John's Gospel. He also taught about the institution of the Eucharist clearly reported in the Gospels of Matthew, Mark, and Luke and in Paul's first letter to the Corinthians, chapters ten and eleven.

In his retreats to the parishes, he began and closed each day with the celebration of the Eucharist. He instructed the pastors and the people to clean their churches and the linens, especially the sanctuary. When he started our community he delivered the same message. Tradition rightly identifies him as the "Apostle of the Eucharist." There is a huge statue of Norbert in St. Peter's Basilica in the Vatican that shows him holding the monstrance containing the Eucharist. Under his right foot is the neck of the heretic Tanchelm, the northern disciple of Berengar.

The artist Peter Paul Rubens created six tapestries celebrating the "Triumph of the Eucharist," one of which shows St. Thomas Aquinas, flanked by St. Norbert on the one side and St. Juliana of Cornillon, who had the vision of the Eucharist that initiated the movement for the feast of Corpus Christi.

In the spiritual and moral renewal of our Order worldwide, these three themes of seeking peace, clerical celibacy, and devotion to the Eucharist still need attention. Norbert emptied himself of his wealth and social standing to found an order of men and women, which by God's grace has endured all these years. Norbert was a living saint. That's our goal too.

Jesus proclaimed and witnessed his gospel to an oral culture. Memory was strong, and while St. Norbert's culture was literate, most people still lived in rural settings where hearing, memory, and oral culture were still prized. In a society where 90 percent of people lived in rural areas, effective preaching and powerful personal witness were the main ways the story of God's plan for our salvation was communicated. Norbert is remembered as a missionary preacher. At Magdeburg he trained other Norbertines to be mission preachers to the Wends a tribe in northeast Germany. The Liturgy of the Hours for the feast of St. Norbert cites his gift:

> Norbert was a most eloquent preacher; after long meditation he would preach the word of God, and with his fiery eloquence purged vices, refined virtues and filled souls of good will with the warmth of wisdom.

> (Liturgy of the Hours, Volume 3, Page 1459)

The Gregorian Reform Inspired St. Norbert

In the eleventh century, the Church's members needed reforms. Corruption resulted from simony and the sale of spiritual benefits and church offices. Another evil was lay investiture, the selection and approval of bishops by emperors and kings, who chose men by secular and political standards and not by their faith in Christ and commitment to Gospel values. God gave the Church Pope Gregory VII (1073–85) to lead the needed reform movement. St. Norbert was inspired by this Gregorian Reform, which led to his founding of our Order. There is a saying that explains the need for reform in religious life: Diligence produces abundance. Abundance leads to laxity. Laxity fosters decline, which cries out for reform.

Pope Gregory VII emphasized the renewal of the spiritual and moral lives of the priesthood, and Norbert responded to this call.

He wanted to put on the "new self" and live a life of perfection in the service of the Church. He would become a priest and live the religious life. For the Gregorian reformers, priesthood joined to religious life represented a unifying principle, the very principle that distinguished the regular canons from secular canons. Religious life would serve the priesthood and thus the Church, since it would be able to promote holiness among the clergy.

The sanctification of the clergy is essential for pastoral service to God's people. In that context, Norbert led an Order dedicated to the greater glory of God, the salvation of souls, and the spread of Christ's kingdom of love, justice, and mercy.

St. Norbert had spent considerable time as a missionary. Now he would embrace the religious life. I consider this his third conversion.

St. Norbert Starts Our Order

In tune with Pope Gregory's reform, guided by the Holy Spirit and the wisdom of the Church, St. Norbert established our community in 1121. He chose a place called Premontré. He envisioned a community of priests, Canons Regular, who would live by the Gospel and the Rule of St. Augustine in response to God's call to holiness. Taking vows of poverty, chastity, and obedience, committed to the choral Divine Office, and centered on the celebration of the Eucharist, the members were to be formed for ministerial service to the local church.

The Norbertines were not monks in the traditional sense, but rather they were oriented toward the care of people in parishes. This was a new form of religious life combining the monastic and pastoral ministry, re-capturing what Augustine did in the fourth century. Eventually brothers and sisters were accepted and invited to this quest for holiness. St. Norbert sought a form of the Apostolic life described in Acts 2:42–47: "They devoted themselves to the Apostles' teaching and to the fellowship, to the breaking of the bread and to prayer. . . . " Norbert's original community was richly blessed from the start. At Premontré, Norbert formed his followers by "Word and Example." He supplemented this with *Lectio Divina*, a slow and patient listening in silence to God's word. He nourished his members with the music of the Psalms in the choir. He celebrated Mass, feeding them with the Word made flesh. He challenged them with Augustine's Rule. That was the spiritual environment from which their voices went forth to all the earth. The first mission of the Norbertines was to supply twelve members to take over Antwerp's St. Michael's Collegiate church and monastery, replacing the twelve canons who denied Christ's real presence in the Eucharist.

St. Norbert loved these words about the first Christians: "They devoted themselves to the breaking of the bread." (Acts 2:42) He made the Mass the center of his spirituality and ministry saying, "It is at the altar that we show our faith and love for God." Everything in the life of St. Norbert and his first disciples highlights the central place of the Eucharist, the heart of the community of Canons Regular at Premontré. The canons surrounded the altar with splendor and solemnity. As a canon formed since his youth in the liturgical atmosphere of Xanten, this led him to use liturgical imagery and the ideal of beauty as a way of giving glory to God.

Along with his love of the Eucharist, St. Norbert had a deep affection for Mary. He often pointed out that the first Christians who prayed for the coming the Holy Spirit, were gathered around Mary. "They devoted themselves to prayer with Mary the mother of Jesus." (Acts

1:14) He dedicated the church at Premontré to Mary and required that Marian feasts be celebrated with special solemnity. Their profound faith in the Eucharist and the role of Mary equipped them to be outstanding examples of salt and light; witnesses to Christ.

Eight years after the founding of our Order, while on a mission recruiting new vocations, Norbert was elected archbishop of Magdeburg. His dream was firmly in place at Premontré. He would create a new Abbey in Magdeburg and encourage missions to that part of the world. Blessed Hugh became our first Abbot and stabilized Norbert's insights, guaranteeing centuries of service to Christ's Church, the salvation of souls, and the apostolic ideal.

CHAPTER FOUR

The Novitiate in Madison, Wisconsin

My first year in spiritual formation

T HE novitiate was set on a ten-acre piece of land bordering Lake Monona. A large white house served as our residence. Nearby was a small barn and a chicken coop. A number of shade trees dotted the land. The property was a gift from an elderly and prosperous Catholic and his two sisters, unmarried and living on a similar lakeside property a half mile away. Our Norbertine Brother Clem Tourangeau lived with them and looked after them. Father Leonard Wagner was our Master of Novices and Brother Paschal was the cook. Our dorm was on the top floor. On the first floor, handsome, wood-carved statues of St. Norbert and St. Augustine stood at the entrance of a wood paneled chapel. Across the hall was our dining room and kitchen, behind which was Brother Paschal's quarters. Inside the front door was a visiting room and a grand piano. Our community room was on the second floor. Father Wagner's quarters were on this floor.

Since quiet was a prevailing part of our training, it

helped that our property was surrounded with farmland and the front road did not have a lot of traffic. As we looked across the lake we could see the domed capitol and, occasionally, sailboats. Our day centered on Mass, the lengthy chanting of the Liturgy of the Hours in Latin, a time for meditation, the rosary, and other devotional prayers, meals, and a morning presentation on the religious life by Father Wagner. Many of the themes he spoke about were drawn from a document called *Opera Diei* (*Works of the Day*).

We were given handwritten copies of the *Opera Diei* done by previous novices and we would write out a copy for our personal use. The topics were about living the essentials of religious life, such as prayer, self- discipline, and the virtues of poverty, chastity, and obedience. There was particular emphasis on devotion to the Eucharist, praise of God, the Liturgy of the Hours, the vows, meditation, and honoring the Virgin Mary. Raised on a farm, Father Wagner often drew applications from his experience to the spiritual topics before us.

Except for Saturday and Sunday, many of our afternoons were occupied with outdoor assignments: cleaning the chicken coop; collecting eggs; mowing the lawns; digging up tree roots; carrying buckets of water from the lake to use on the strawberry patches and raspberry bushes; wrapping harvested apples individually in newspaper for further use in winter; taking the feathers off the chickens Brother Paschal had killed; and shoveling snow from the driveway during the cold Wisconsin winters.

We also washed windows, dusted, cleaned rooms, and washed dishes.

After supper we spent time in our community room usually playing cards or other games or talking and joking about our experiences that day. There was a study period in late afternoon just before Evening Prayer. One of our winter activities was taking the ice sailboat out for a ride on the frozen lake when the ice was firm and free of heavy snow. It was cold but liberating since we normally could not leave the property but were free to do this.

While I chronicle all these activities I should emphasize that we were expected to learn what was called "recollection," turning our minds and hearts to God's presence before, during, and after whatever task with which we were occupied. I recall a prayer that helped me in this: "Dear God I offer you this task for your greater honor and glory, the salvation of souls and the spread of God's kingdom." But sticking to this inner discipline was not easy. I found it hard to settle down and leave behind me the distracting life of the past. To acquire an inner attentiveness to God was slow in coming. In a sense I did not even realize I had an inner life. I don't recall any of us talking about it. Of course the lack of distractions helped and the rhythm of lots of prayer time and work time gradually led us to settle down. The hours of silence stilled our tongues. The quiet became normal. The absence of visitors except once a month for family visits curbed our need for distraction. The reasons for it all began to sink in.

In the second half of the year, things began to click. We had a visit from a legendary Abbot General, Hubert Noots, who was aggressive with Abbeys that needed to conform more faithfully to the traditions of the Order. Each of us met with him. In my conversation he mentioned that in our spiritual reading we should be cautious about books in which the authors spent most of the time on extensive visions of Christ and other mystical experiences. While I was not interested in such literature, I had picked up a book by a Canadian nun that might fit the case. I scanned it a bit, but soon lost interest.

More importantly, he recommended that I read the autobiography of St. Therese of Lisieux, *Story of a Soul.* I followed his advice, and her story helped me at last to seek a personal relationship with Christ. The sense of an interior life finally opened up to me. The road to integrating my religious and everyday duties with my interior life with God began to happen.

I received the gift of God's presence that I had read about and now actually experienced. Fortunately, I also came across a saying that stayed with me. "Do not seek the consolations of God, but rather the God of consolations." As a group we did not discuss this openly, but I found it easy to talk it over with Henry Jafolla, who seemed to have a much more mature appreciation of this than I had. I drew confidence from his encouragement and began to stay with prayer in both the easy and hard times. I often dwelt on St. Therese's insistence on filling each event with the love the Spirit gives us.

Later I read how Mother Teresa of Calcutta framed this teaching. "I am not called to do great things, rather I am summoned to do small things with great love." I also found a quote in Romans 5:5 that summed it up: "The love of God has been poured into our hearts by the Holy Spirit who has been given to us." When Therese discovered her vocation to the love in the heart of the Church, she said, "If this love had disappeared, the apostles would no longer preach the Gospel and the martyrs would refuse to shed their blood."

One of the advantages of the seclusion of the novitiate is that we learned how to get along and become a community. In a sense we became a new family and the relationships that occurred survived into the years ahead. Once again, God brought me, shorn of brothers and sisters, to a brotherhood that I have treasured ever since. One such member of our brotherhood, Glen Siebers, from Appleton, Wisconsin, joined us in October. He had completed two years of college and had entered a diocesan seminary but left after two months and was accepted into our community. He would become a high school teacher in our community for most of his life. Years later, his nephew, Tim Shillcox, joined our Order and is a distinguished pastor in our diocese.

Becoming a Temporary Cathedral Choir

A novitiate does not lend itself to much excitement, but just before Lent in 1947 when the pope created the

Diocese of Madison and placed Bishop O'Connor at the helm. With Holy Week approaching, he needed singers who could do the Latin and Gregorian Chant. He turned to us. Father Vincent De Leers had moved into our house while he pursued studies at the University of Wisconsin. He loved chant and trained us to sing numerous Latin psalms, hymns, and antiphons for the liturgies of the Blessing of the Oils, Holy Thursday, Good Friday, and the Easter Vigil. With that expert training and the high motivation to participate in the Sacred Triduum of Holy Week, we had a satisfying faith experience and were able to help the diocese at the same time.

After our weekend of chant, we returned to regular life at the novitiate until August 12, 1947, when we drove to De Pere for the blessing of Sylvester Killeen as Coadjutor Abbot of our community. To accommodate the crowd, the ceremony took place in the college gym. It was a sunny, hot and humid day, exacerbated by a building filled with people. Cakes of ice with electric fans behind them were mounted near the provisional altar and Father Killeen was sweating so much that Bishop O'Connor shouted, "Throw that man some towels!" We all survived and enjoyed a festive dinner. We returned to Monona Drive where we spent one more week before bidding goodbye to the first year novitiate. Next we attended a retreat that prepared the whole community for the celebration of St. Augustine's Day, August 28, and the vesting of new men and vow ceremonies for the older ones.

The Founding of Our American Norbertine Community

The election of a new abbot allows me to share with you the story of the founding of our community by Father Bernard Pennings. In the early 1890s a renegade Catholic priest, René Vilatte was ordained a bishop of the schismatic Old Catholic Church. He settled in the peninsula just north of Green Bay, where he began to lure Belgian Catholics away from the true Church. The Catholic bishop of Green Bay, Sebastian Messmer, wrote a letter to the Norbertine Abbey of Berne in Holland for help in saving the Catholics from the deceitful work of Villatte. The Dutch abbot agreed and sent Father Pennings along with Father Broens and Brother Heesackers as missionaries to the diocese of Green Bay.

Their ship arrived in Hoboken, New Jersey, on November 13, 1893, the feast of All Saints of the Norbertine Order. When they arrived in Green Bay, they were welcomed by Bishop Messmer who explained his pastoral problem. They immediately moved into parishes at the heart of the Belgian community. The following year, Berne Abbey sent five more members to help with the mission.

In these years the Norbertines made every effort to strengthen the faith of those who had not been led astray and worked even more enthusiastically to win back those whom Villatte had converted. So well did Father Pennings and his team achieve their goal that the *Catholic Citizen* newspaper reported on February 19, 1898, "Vilatte has been left flockless, churchless and landless." But God's grace never left this priest alone until he repented, returned to the Church, and retired to a residence near a Norbertine Abbey in France where he died in 1929.

The Vilatte crisis now over, Father Pennings sought to establish a house for the Order in which native priests could be trained to carry on the mission. The opportunity presented itself when St. Joseph's Church in West De Pere became available. It was officially a shrine to St. Joseph and published a magazine, the *Annals of St. Joseph*. Father Pennings applied for control of the parish and the bishop agreed. Father Pennings arrived with Father Broens, two Norbertine seminarians, and Brother Gilbert. On Wednesday, September 28, 1898, at a Solemn High Mass, the Order of St. Norbert was formally established in the United States at St. Joseph's Shrine with Father Pennings as Prior and Father Broens as Pastor.

They immediately announced that they would accept and train students for the priesthood. Twelve days later Frank Van Dyke received his first Latin lesson from Prior Pennings. Anthony Vissers enrolled a week later. By November, Charles Savageau and Bill Marchant arrived. All four persevered and were ordained priests.

This humble beginning is recorded as the beginning of St. Norbert College. Their growth was not without difficulty. They were faced with rough Wisconsin winters, learning English, and adapting to American culture. But the deep faith of the founders provided the firm foundation in parish ministry and Catholic education and the steps toward Abbey life in the new world. Pennings was named an Abbot in 1925 and retained that office until his death in 1955.

CHAPTER FIVE

College Education and Theological Training

I N September 1947, we high school graduates began our college education at St. Norbert's. We were expected to pursue a double major, one in philosophy and one in our teaching preference for which I chose English. In the little house-chapel we chanted Matins, Lauds, and Vespers and attended daily Mass. On Wednesday nights we chanted the Seven Penitential Psalms. Privately, we prayed the Little Office of the Blessed Virgin. Our title was Frater (brother) but usually we were called frats. In those days, the priests celebrated private Masses which we took turns serving. In the dining room we generally ate in silence while a Frater read from the Rule of St. Augustine or some other religious book. Conversation was permitted for Sunday lunch and supper and on some other special occasions.

Most of the time, when we ate in silence, there was a buzz from knives, forks and spoons and shuffling of servers collecting the plates. But one day that changed dramatically. Suddenly, the dining room was filled with palpable quiet. The reader had begun with chapter one of Thomas Merton's captivating autobiography, *Seven Storey Mountain*. I still recall the impact of Merton's absorbing story and the undivided attention it received from all of us. Merton's subsequent writings on prayer and the development of a social conscience influenced many of us.

There were about thirty of us in formation. The older men briefed us on the professors and the courses. Time for exercise was allotted on Wednesday, Saturday, and Sunday afternoons. I joined the hikers for the three-mile walk to the Sanitarium on Saturdays where we visited the sick. I learned to play singles tennis, a game I stayed with until I was seventy. In the winter I tried to play ice hockey, but the locals were too good at it, so I just kept walking.

I started to smoke a pipe, a custom I retained until I was sixty-five when my doctor and dentist pestered me to stop. Besides that our buildings became smoke free. I was surprised that I had virtually no trouble in giving up the pipe.

I felt most at home in my English classes and became a disciple of Father Pat Butler, a legendary Norbertine English professor. In those days Great Books programs were popular and suited my major as well. Mortimer Adler was the chief exponent of this program and wrote the influential *How to Read a Book*, which I devoured and from which I learned much. I resolved to read a book a week and stuck with that habit for many years. I still read a lot of history, biography, spiritual works, and the occasional novel. I owe all those authors who engaged

me thanks for their insights, imagination, and desire to
share themselves through writing. Though I now get dis-
tracted by TV, Netflix, and email, occasions that eat up
one's reading time, I am working on keeping reading a
priority.

Our newly ordained Father Bob Brooks had been a
leader among the frats in taking spiritual reading seriously. For a time, he was an informal spiritual director
for a number of us. While I did not seek his spiritual
guidance I was impressed by his love of the writings of
Abbot Marmion. Very soon I acquired a habit of reading Marmion's two books, *Christ the Ideal of the Monk*
and *Christ in His Mysteries*, every year of my seminary
training and some years after that. Marmion was an Irish
diocesan seminarian who studied in Rome and was captivated by the Benedictine priests he met with their love
of liturgy as the primary source of spiritual development.

So enthusiastic was Marmion about that Order that
after his ordination in Dublin, he requested his bishop
to allow him to join the Benedictines. The bishop told
him to wait five years, and if he still felt that way, then
he would be let go. That's what happened. After a number of years as a monk he began writing his two seminal
books. Marmion's ability to unify scripture, liturgy, and
spirituality was impressive and attractive. Moreover, I
was moved by his capacity to make Christ a real person,
accessible through the Bible and the Eucharist.

Marmion especially loved the letters of St. Paul whom
he cited continually in Latin. Of all the spiritual writers

I found inspiring, Marmion was the best. He knew how to invite me into meeting Christ in a personal way. In later life, when I was doing catechetical work, my affinity for scripture and liturgy was always evident. Years later when I was a professor at Blessed John XXIII Seminary, I joined our pilgrimage to Rome for the beatification of Blessed John XXIII and my revered spiritual guide, the great Abbot Marmion.

My first one-week vacation back home was a joyful, tearful reunion with Mom. Abbot Killeen had visited her and told me that she needed help. I was prepared to leave when my Cousin Catherine called and told me that she and her husband Frank had brought her to their home. I was deeply moved by their loving generosity. Mom lived one more year before going to our heavenly Father. I remained eternally grateful to Catherine and Frank and always spent my vacation time with them and their growing family whom I still see every year for the week before Christmas and the day itself.

We were expected to complete college in three years, taking many courses each semester and over the summer. Somehow we did it and graduated with class of 1950. While I found English a ready-made topic for my interests, I struggled with philosophy, until I joined a study group reading the *Summa Theologica* of St. Thomas Aquinas led by one of my friends, Frater Brendan McKeough. While it is a theological work, it is filled with philosophical insight. As one frat said to me, "Al, when you take theology you will see the value of philosophy."

That proved to be true. Much later I read a book by Father Robert Barron, *Thomas Aquinas, Spiritual Director,* which further expanded Aquinas' breadth and depth, showing the integral connection between spirituality, philosophy, and theology. Barron demonstrated how the *Summa* is a dramatic story of the ecstasy of God emptying himself in Christ for our salvation, and how the ecstasy of Jesus in the process of returning to the Father is a journey he makes possible for us in union with him. In other words, Aquinas behaved as a spiritual guide and not just a dry theological writer. Good theology and sound spirituality are blood brothers.

With this reflection, I journey with you into my theological training, all of which took place at the Abbey and with Norbertine professors. I also began my first years as a high school teacher at St. Norbert High School. Half the students were boarders and the other half were day students, mostly from De Pere. I was assigned to two classes of junior English which was actually a survey of American literature along with continued study of grammar and composition. In the beginning, it was challenging. I was a green teacher and a disciplinarian. I had thirty-five boys in each class, guys whose interest in the Green Bay Packers far outstripped their interest in Emily Dickinson. When I recited the first line of her poem, "I'm Nobody" they quickly said, "Yea frat!" Many an alumnus reminds me that my anger showed up in a bright red face, and being short and thin, I was not able to impress them with a formidable build.

I learned the rules of teaching the hard way. Be well prepared. Tell them what is expected of them and hold them responsible. Learn the lesson of the stare. When you are that self-confident, you will succeed. The second year and beyond went well. I became comfortable with the teenagers' give and take, and even began to enjoy it. One of my greatest memories as a teacher happened four years later when I was a priest. I encouraged the students to read a short book every two weeks. At the end of that time I devoted one class in which they finished reading the last chapters while I went to each student and talked with him about what he was reading.

One student was Charley Swanson, whose claim to fame was that his grandmother was the cook for the famed Von Trapp Family Singers whose story was told in *The Sound of Music*. He had been reading a collection of Thomas Merton's poetry, *The Tears of the Blind Lions*. I asked him what he thought of it. He looked up at me and from memory he said, "Father, your ecstasy is your apostolate, for whom to kick is *contemplata tradere*." I was astounded. He had quoted the best line from the poem, "The Quickening of John the Baptist." The line refers to baby John leaping in the womb of Elizabeth in the presence of baby Jesus in the womb of Mary. Merton compared John's ecstasy to a monk who leaps with contemplative joy in meeting Jesus. It is in such spiritual joy that the radiance of the monastic life nurtures the faith of the people of our Church.

* * *   * * *   * * *

During my undergraduate years I was also impressed with Father Steinmetz who taught Dogma and was exactly the right man for the mission. A dedicated hunter and fisherman, he looked big and strong and spoke with a quiet voice. He rarely looked at notes, demonstrating a mastery of the various doctrines set before us. Unlike many of our teachers, he thrived on questions, coming alive with the boldest challenges and riding steadily along like a great ship moving smoothly through the waters. He had a knack of taking a difficult-to-grasp Latin phrase such as God being *ipsum esse subsistens* in such a way that this mystery of God became accessible to us. While I didn't always get it, I did learn that these lofty descriptions of God are not threatening but friendly invitations to having a relationship with God.

We all knew that "Steiny," as we called him, was a rabid fisherman, and that, standing before us, just as he scanned the surfaces of Wisconsin lakes for the bubbles that signaled a trout, his penetrating gaze wandered over us searching for an inner light among us. I don't know how often I presented a dull face, but I know that I possessed an eagerness to hear his theological and faith-filled insights which still govern my catechetical work. In what was to be my last goodbye with him on the evening of my departure to Catholic University as a visiting professor, he counseled me, "You will face much opposition. Don't let them get you down." I did not see him again for he died while I was in Washington. I often needed his

insights, but God did send other wisdom speakers into
my life.

I was also fond of Father Albin, a Hungarian
Norbertine priest who fled the Communist takeover of
his country just after completing his doctoral studies in
moral theology in Rome. He was brilliant without sound-
ing that way because he could take the starkest moral
problem with a wit and humor that shaved it down to
everyday wisdom in perfect tune with the Church's traditions. I wish I had copied down his endless stream of witty
stories that took the pompous language of famous mor-
alists and reduced them to the headaches of a humanity
ever striving to live up to ideals and just as easily falling
again.

Albin always defended our traditions but not with
ominous threats about our human weaknesses. He per-
sonified the mercy of God and Christ's tireless efforts
to hurry with forgiveness to the side of every sinner. He
wandered our streets looking for those who hunger for
mercy, stopping by the fallen and saying, "Here, let me
help you up." For Albin, moral theology was a melody of
mercy, the music of angels, God's gift of a Catholicism
that has lasted 2000 years. In his vision, no sin was ever
so great that Jesus could not wash it away from a penitent
seeking forgiveness.

That particular semester the principal had put a
notice on our bulletin board asking for someone to teach
religion to the freshmen. I went right over to his office and
volunteered. He accepted my offer and I began teaching

them surveys of the Old and New Testaments. The fruit of my efforts was eventually put into a book I wrote, *A Guide to the Bible*. I obtained some background from a Bible library on the second floor of the Abbey. Eventually I found out that the collection could be traced back to a much beloved Norbertine theology professor, Father Gregory Rybrook, a brilliant Roman-trained Dutchman who also served as prior and other house offices during the years.

Our teachers often quoted him and his sense of humor. I grazed his shelves of books and found some useful stories, examples, and explanations of scripture. So, between theology classes and high school teaching, my time of preparation for priesthood sped inexorably toward the goal of ordination that suddenly came upon me. While studying and teaching absorbed our attention and energies, time had its own rules and before we knew it, the bells were ringing for priesthood.

CHAPTER SIX

Ordination and First Mass

Priestly Ministry

> O my God, if I cannot say at every moment that
> I love you, let my heart say it for me with every
> breath I take.
>
> —St. John Vianney,
> Curé of Ars and patron of all priests

IN 1953 it was time for ordinations. Since five of us were from Philadelphia we were given permission to be ordained in St. Edmond's parish church, to which Vince Conway, Henry Jafolla, and Bob Kelly belonged. I was from St. Patrick's and John Cox came from St. Gabriel's. St. Edmond's was a comparatively new church and seated a thousand people. It was filled. Archbishop O'Hara, soon to be a cardinal, ordained us. The two things I recall from ordination was lying face down on the floor of the sanctuary while the choir sang the litany of saints and then the brief gesture of the archbishop making me a priest by putting his hands firmly on my head. That did it, along with ordination prayers that accompanied that ancient ceremony: I was a priest.

My first Mass was at St. Patrick's. The pastor, Father James Vallely, stood by me to help me through the ceremony, to keep me calm, and to be sure I didn't miss something. It was 98 degrees with no air conditioning, and I was clothed in vestments that were heavy with gold thread. I was hot and tense and nervous, but I had veteran priests around me to get me through it. Father Horn, our youth priest, served as deacon and the Norbertine Father Joseph Dorff was subdeacon. St. Patrick's famed men and boys choir sang one of their best Masses: Licinio Refice's *Missa Choralis* in which he used the soaring melody of what was called the "Great Amen" that was designed to lift our spirits. It certainly did for me that day.

The highlight of my first Mass was when I recited the words of Christ that consecrated the bread and wine, which became his body and blood. Because of God's graces, I still feel awe at every consecration I offer at every Mass. In giving my First Blessings right after Mass, I approached the people who knelt at the altar rail as though at Communion. I was filled with emotion as I saw friend after friend whom I had not seen for eight years. When I saw Mr. McNulty, still the secretary of the St. Vincent De Paul Society, weeping openly, I was overwhelmed. I thought gratefully of all those food checks for McGonagle's store that our family received from his efforts. For the festive dinner, my cousin Catherine found a restaurant called the Homestead in a brownstone house facing Rittenhouse Square. They served a family style meal at a very reasonable cost. A good time was had by all.

Priestly Ministry

A week after the festivities I returned to the Abbey with my classmates. I was now called a "simplex" priest, meaning I had one more year of theology to study. I was not yet permitted to hear confessions or preach. Our class moved to the Villa where we began seven years before. Father Hockers was our house master. We continued to participate in the Liturgy of the Hours. We offered a daily private Mass and attended theology courses. Instead of recreating with the frats, we were invited to socialize with the priests in their community room.

On Sundays I took a bus to Neenah where I would celebrate the ten-thirty and noon Masses at St. Margaret Mary's, an attractive, tasteful neo-gothic church, with a good deal of mahogany wood trim. The pastor was Monsignor Glueckstein. His sisters Christine and Hildegarde did the cooking and the bookkeeping respectively. Father Willard McKinnon was the assistant priest. The pastor, a cheerful, kindly, friendly man, set the tone. The two eighth-grade servers were unusually tall and enjoyed towering over me. They both became priests: Bill Kuhr for the diocese and Gene Griese for the Norbertines. It was a great first assignment that shaped my attitude to ministry.

In those days, Catholics fasted from food and drink from midnight until Mass was complete. In reality, I had fasted from supper time the day before to 1:00 p.m. on Sunday. So when Christine put a big breakfast in front of me, I wolfed it down. Better yet, she served Sunday dinner at two o'clock and I feasted again. The three Norbertines who had Masses in Oshkosh would arrive around two-thirty to pick me up for the drive back to the Abbey.

My Carmelite Prayer Sisters

St. Therese of Lisieux included in her prayer life the fundamental needs of priests. She was attracted to St. Paul's vision of the Church as the Body of Christ as he developed it in his first letter to the Corinthians. "You are Christ's body, and individually parts of it." (1 Cor 12:12–21) St. Paul knew that the Christian life was a great mystery. There are forces affecting us that we barely recognize. He tries to capture that truth with his teachings about the Mystical Body of Christ. We are all linked to one another in the Body of Christ. A personal experience of this was my gift of "prayer partners."

Carmelite cloistered nuns are called to be power houses of prayer on behalf of the Church and its priests, following the example of St. Therese. One of the first things I did after my ordination was to write to the Carmelite Sisters in Sioux City, Iowa. I asked them for the gift of a sister prayer partner for blessings on my priestly ministry and the virtue of perseverance. I received that gift in the person of Sister Gabriel Dolan. May God bless her. For the next twenty-five years she sent prayers to God on my behalf. Two years before her death, I happened to be in the diocese to speak to the Catholic school teachers.

The superintendent knew about my link to Sister Gabriel and arranged for me to meet her. It was a joyful occasion. I asked what she did before joining the Carmelites. She said "I played basketball on my high school team." That light-hearted and down-to-earth reply touched me. Privately, I prayed I would have that holy earthiness twenty-five years into my priesthood. I am currently sixty years a priest and still trailing Sister Gabriel in holy earthiness.

After her death, I entreated the prioress for another prayer partner. I was given Sister Therese of the Spirit of Love. We became good personal friends. In time she became the prioress and invited me for an annual reflection weekend for the sisters. I believe that weekend was more fruitful for me than for those marvelous sisters. After twenty-five more years with Sister Therese as my prayer partner, she suffered an early death. I attended her funeral and, at the burial, stopped by Sister Gabriel's grave to bless her and thank her again. Presently, I have the gift of Sister Jeanne Marie. I feel close to her since her family is from Wisconsin. I happen to be writing these words on the feast of Our Lady of Mount Carmel, a liturgical celebration of one of the greatest religious orders in the Church.

My Full Time Ministry Begins

My son, you are about to be advanced to the order of the presbyterate (priesthood). You must

apply your energies to the duty of teaching in
the name of Christ, the chief teacher. Meditate
on the law of God. Believe what you read. Teach
what you believe. Put into practice what you
teach.

(Bishop's address to candidate for priesthood.
The Rites, Volume 2, page 40.)

Those words of Archbishop O'Hara on the day of my
ordination in 1954 assumed a realistic vitality when I
began my full dedication to priestly ministry. At the completion of my simplex year, I was assigned to be an assistant
at St. Joseph's parish that served the Abbey, the college,
and the high school. The pastor was Abbot Pennings, but
the acting pastor was Father Charles Killeen, the brother
of the Coadjutor Abbot. I also taught classes at the high
school. My parish duties included Masses at the church,
confessions on Saturdays, training the altar servers, taking sick-calls, bringing Communion to the bed-ridden
on First Fridays, anointing the sick, conducting funerals,
and blessing marriages.

Like all new posts, it took time to get used to the various responsibilities, but I was young (just twenty-five),
energetic, and a quick learner. Father Killeen was easy
to approach with questions. Since I was already familiar with the Church and its diverse audiences due to my
seven years of training, the role of an assistant priest was
made easier.

I remember my first sick call. I drove to a farm house

that looked like a log cabin. I was led into the bedroom where a man lay very ill. He was breathing heavily, and to my inexperienced eyes he seemed at death's door. His wife knelt by him. After I finished the anointing I suggested we say the rosary. I was nervous and did not yet have the pastoral skills of comforting her and her husband. I left after that. I heard later that the man recovered and lived many more years.

On St. Patrick's Day, I was in my room preparing a homily when I heard the church bell toll. I noticed the contrast of the bell and the metallic toll of the pile driver that was currently laying the foundation of a new theater on the campus that was to be named Abbot Pennings Hall. Our ninety-three-year-old Abbot had died. One toll of the church bell announced his death, while the clang of the pile driver proclaimed the erection of a monument in his honor. From 1893, when he arrived in America, to 1955, Abbot Pennings was an apostle to the people in this part of the world, proclaiming and witnessing the Gospel of Christ in a great variety of ways.

Abbot Killeen announced that there would be three funerals. The first one was for the children and I was called to preach the sermon. I was used to the children by then and began by contrasting two tolling sounds. The next day was set aside as the funeral for the members of St. Joseph parish. Only a few people could attend because Mother Nature provided a twenty-inch snow blizzard that paralyzed the community. Father Killeen tried vainly to clear some of the snow away, but the wind had other plans. But by the afternoon the sun came out and the temperature grew so warm that the snow melted considerably. On the following day, the third funeral Mass at the Cathedral was packed with priests, the bishop, the Norbertines, and many others.

* * *   * * *   * * *

My second year at the parish was marked by the appointment of Father Blaise Peters as pastor. He was well known as a dynamic priest, filled with energy and prepared to serve the people with all his heart. God blessed me with such a priest as a mentor. He showed me how to serve people far more effectively than I could have hoped. He led by example, tirelessly hearing confessions and visiting the sick at their homes and in the nearby hospitals and nursing homes. In the first two years he visited virtually every home and apartment where parishioners lived, desiring to serve them as much as possible.

At nights he was in his office, giving marriage preparation, instructions to converts, saving marriages, and consoling troubled people. In my case he developed the custom of setting aside the first half hour after supper for visiting with me. He asked me about my day and made useful comments. He invited me to ask him about his day and to make my own observations. This happened usually five evenings a week, for the next four years, barring vacations and other interruptions. I learned from him what mentoring means and benefitted from his wisdom.

Of the many experiences at this parish, I will not forget

the night of a parish party that was part fund raiser and part entertainment held in our school hall. Mrs. McCabe of the women's society was in charge. She was short of change and sent her daughter Eileen back to their home for more. Time passed. Then her son, Vincent, came in, took me aside, and said that Eileen was just killed in an automobile crash while crossing highway 41. He wanted me to tell his mother. Usually, Father Peters was there, but something had caused him to be away from the parish. I asked Vincent to go over to the rectory and wait in the living room. I stressed that he should not come out but wait until we were there. I told Mrs. McCabe there was a phone call for her and I would take her to the rectory to receive the message.

I had escorted her halfway there when Vincent came out shouting, "Mother! Eileen has been killed in an accident!" I felt her beginning to fall, but got Vincent to help me with her while we brought her inside. Vincent gave her the details. We did our best to console her and pray together. The funeral was heart breaking. In time, a vigil light stand was installed underneath the pulpit in our church: "In Loving Memory of Eileen McCabe."

During these years I also taught classes at the high school. One of my students, Steve, had a severe stuttering problem. I had heard that memorizing easy poetry and little stories sometimes helped to subdue the stutter. I proposed that he come to the rectory where I would take him through a few easy recitations. We started with "This is the house that Jack built . . ." He willingly tried this and other similar readings, but I did not see any improvements and felt I was not helping him. I had read that there was a speech therapy program at the University of Iowa and suggested he use the summer to go there. He didn't return to our school the next year.

Some years later on a spring evening I was told I had a visitor. It was Steve. In gloriously perfect pronunciation with not a glimmer of a stutter, he easily said, "Hello Father McBride, I'm happy to see you." A lengthy conversation followed in which he explained his experiences at the University of Iowa's Wendell Johnson Speech and Hearing Clinic. Steve was finally confident in speaking without any apparent problems. His story was heartwarming and I praised God for the outcome. I never saw him again, but was heartened nonetheless. I know that most teachers have an even greater collection of similar stories, in which they were instruments of hope for special students. God bless them.

As I reflect upon my decades as a priest, I praise God that my first years were serving in a parish and teaching high school boys. I learned how to teach and came to the conclusion that in order to be effective my preaching should be a teaching moment. In 1950 Bishop Sheen began his remarkable TV shows. For a half hour each week he captivated millions of Catholics, Protestants, Jews, and many unbelievers. What I saw, right away, was a fabulous teacher at work. He used a blackboard, but no notes.

Bishop Sheen scored one point each episode,

meaning that his talks were not like buckshot, splashing ideas everywhere, but more like one solid bullet, driving the message home. He always began with a corny joke, followed by a story that carried his point. Usually, three developments of the one message followed. With his hypnotic eyes and voice, he soared with emotion. He finished each lesson with the salutation "God Love You." A good preacher should be a good teacher. He also proved that a teacher can be holy and the Vatican has confirmed that truth by declaring him "Venerable," the first of three steps toward canonization.

My early years as a high school teacher, and the example of Bishop Sheen played a major role in how I would approach preaching and the priesthood over the years to come.

I also thank the Lord for my four years of training in St. Joseph parish with mentors like Fathers Killeen and Peters. The basic lesson that the parish life taught me was the vitality of the faith of our people. I felt faith in the life of Mrs. McCabe, even in the heat of the news that her daughter was killed. Faith in God lifted her during the worst moment of her life. The faith of our Catholic people is best experienced in parish life. I was later to face a lot of challenges to my personal faith when at times it seemed to be collapsing around me. I am sorry to say I was never as strong as I would like to think I am. I recall a moment in my life when I endured some intractable problems in my ministry, and a faith-filled parish member lifted me up.

I had just finished Sunday Mass and my inner turmoil at the time was apparently on display. An Irish woman, a member of the Legion of Mary, approached me, put her hand on my shoulder, and said, "Father McBride, God will never give you a burden you can't carry so long as you seek his help." The faith of that good woman poured into my heart so I could carry on. Four years of being lifted up by hundreds of blessings of faith from the members grounded me for the years that lay ahead. A teaching priest without faith is empty. A teaching priest penetrated with faith is a subtle fire storm.

CHAPTER SEVEN

CHAPTER SEVEN

Novice Master

St. Augustine's "Little Sayings"

Where humility reigns, there is love. When does
    prayer fall silent?

When desire grows cold. It is better to love and be
    hard, than to be gentle and cause harm.

It is better to need less than to have more.

Don't let your garb be noticeable. Seek not by
    clothing , but by lifestyle to please.

Do not claim your mind is pure when your eyes
    are impure. Impure eyes are the sign of an
    impure heart.

You can measure your progress by your growth
    in concern for the common good, rather than
    your private good.

Do not let your mouths alone take food, but let
    also your ears be hungry.

—Quoted with sources in Augustine's homilies
and his Rule, by Thomas Martin, O.S.A.,
"Our Restless Hearts," pp. 67–69

Abbot Killeen appointed me to novice master at our newly
opened Abbey in August 1959. I had no idea this would

happen and it never occurred to me that I would receive this responsibility. Father Peters was not pleased; he had already planned to have me enter Catholic University in Washington, DC, for a summer school program for people engaged in parish Confraternity of Christian Doctrine (CCD) ministry. I would have enjoyed that, but, in those days, a dialogue about appointments was rare. This was the abbot's decision and I would do what he told me. I knew I would miss the parish and the evening chats with Father Peters. When he retired at seventy, he took a job as chaplain at the Catholic hospital in Eureka where he worked until his death, fifteen years later. I enjoyed visiting him several times over those years and preached his funeral at the Abbey.

All throughout my seminary training, we heard the Rule of Augustine, an enduring and persuasive collection of the wisdom of Augustine, every week during meals, a custom, alas, currently tabled in our community. I was familiar with the great saint, but during my term of office I would need to allude to Augustine's role in our formation. So, when I assumed the role of novice master I began reading books by and about Augustine. Throughout my extensive reading of Augustine, the thing that stuck with me the most was his great love for the Psalms.

Peter Brown, in my favorite book about St. Augustine, *Augustine of Hippo*, echoed Augustine's sentiment:

> The Psalms were the record of the emotions of
> Christ and his members. Just as he had taken on

human flesh, so Christ himself had, of his own
free will, opened himself to human feeling . . .
His voice in the Psalms, a voice singing hap-
pily, a voice groaning, a voice rejoicing in hope,
sighing in its present state, we should know this
voice thoroughly, feel it intimately, make it our
own.

Brown also notes Augustine's love of the of the rhythmic
chants of the North African farmers at harvest times and
he is moved to think of the vision of God:

Men who sing like this—in the harvest, at the
grape picking, in any task that totally absorbs
them—may begin by showing their contentment
in songs with word; but they soon become filled
with such a happiness that they can no longer
express it in words, and, leaving aside syllables,
strike up a wordless chant of jubilation.

(Peter Brown, *Augustine of Hippo*, University of
California Angeles Press, 257–8)

* * *   * * *   * * *

At this time, I was also appointed to assist Father Neitzel,
who was in charge of the formation of all the Fraters at
the Abbey, with the second-year novices. Abbot Killeen
had already commissioned the building of a new Abbey
building on a tract of land donated to us by Victor
McCormack. The Abbot told me that I would become

novice master when the new Abbey opened, just a year away.

To prepare me for this new task, I was sent to the Madison novitiate, this time to be tutored by Father Wagner on the requirements for the formation of novices. In the same setting where I did my novitiate, I now viewed it from the other side. I thank God for the graces of teaching religion to young people and also for parish experience with faith-filled people and a pastor who was, as Jesus wished, "A Good Shepherd." These two streams of spirituality gave me a perspective that guided me in formation.

One of the special ministries of the Abbey was the Sunday 11:00 a.m. radio Mass sponsored by the Norbertine radio station, WBAY. The history behind this development began around 1925. The idea of developing a radio station started as an experiment by the Physics Club at St. Norbert College. It became a commercial radio station that, by 1935, was described as "the ideal one hundred watts station in this country." Father Jimmy Wagner emerged as its leader and, eventually, the 10:00 a.m. radio Mass was born. The prominent preachers during my time at St. Joseph's were Fathers Anselm Keefe and Patrick Butler who celebrated the Masses and gave the sermons. Not only were they lions of the college staff, but they were also excellent preachers. In my last year at the parish, I was asked to assume this responsibility. After the first year, I occasionally received letters requesting copies of the talks. A collection of these sermons provided the material for my first published book, *Homilies for the New Liturgy.*

The radio format led me to create many rules for my preaching. I believed that finding an appropriate story to start the homily was important for gaining the attention of the congregation. While I often faltered from this ideal, I did have some success in linking the story with the message of the scripture readings or texts from the liturgy and the experience of the audience.

My memory was relatively strong in those days, so I delivered the homily without notes. I felt that eye contact with the people was an essential part of the communication. As their attention became apparent, their energy fed my own and increased the effectiveness of the talks.

Furthermore, due to radio requirements, I limited my presentation to ten minutes so that the sung Mass could conclude at two minutes to eleven. That discipline has served me well throughout my priesthood. The ten-minute habit became so ingrained in me that I rarely broke the rule.

Finally, I made sure I knew how I would end the homily. Often, I simply memorized the last sentence and ended there, no matter where I was, when I reached ten minutes. While this sometimes caused me to leave things out, it ensured that I reiterated the central point.

Now, that was all technique. The major issue of any homily is preaching the content of the faith and how it applies to the lives of the listeners. All of my education and life experience is meant to supply and apply the Word of God to our people so their faith and life is deepened. Given my youth at that time—I was in my late twenties—I had a long way to go before I possessed the wisdom for which my listeners hungered. Fortunately, I am an inveterate reader. I devoured books on scripture, liturgy, doctrine, and morality. As an English major, I also found immense value in literature. The wisdom of poets and durable fiction touches the heart. Scripture in the Liturgy of the Hours and prayer fed my faith and has never ceased to do so.

In recent years I have paid more attention to the writings of the Fathers of the Church. They have a remarkable capacity to probe the depths of scripture and to powerfully apply God's revelation to people of any age. My four volumes of the Liturgy of the Hours are filled with underlined passages and written references to memorable quotes, mostly from the Fathers.

My second year at the Madison novitiate was a time of great expectations. Father Wagner was generous in sharing with me the wisdom he had gained and readily advised me when I had problems. With the dawn of a new Abbey, the spirits of the community were naturally uplifted. Abbot Killeen embodied the hopes and joys all embraced.

The New Abbey

> From the choir and altar, we go to serve the
> human family
> In a spirit of simplicity, hospitality, reconciliation
> and peace for the benefit of the Church and
> of the world,
> especially where Christ is found among the poor,
> the suffering and among those who do not
> know him.
> We pray that what God's Spirit has begun in us,
> May be made perfect in the day of Christ Jesus.
>
> —From our Vision Statement

Since starting my novitiate, I had grown accustomed to the Midwest and to the Norbertines. I grew to appreciate the role of structure in the training of the seminarians. That would become more evident at the new Abbey when formation was transferred there and it would supplement defects in my role as novice master, due either to my lack of experience or to the intractable sides of human nature.

Ground was broken for the new Abbey, June 9, 1956, and Abbot Killeen led the community to its new Abbey on February 1, 1959. I was midway through the last year of the Madison novitiate. The community settled into a new building and a new phase of communal, liturgical, and prayer life. The whole Latin Office and the use of full Norbertine rituals was being fulfilled. The community found itself in a largely monastic environment.

This was not the practice of the Abbey at the time of its inception in 1925. De Pere's experience had been shaped by parish and school ministries in far flung places like Philadelphia, Delaware, Montana, Green Bay, Madison, Chicago, and Door County. The ideal sought in 1959 was to bring the community together in one place. It didn't work. Members in schools gradually returned to their priories. Members in parishes, of course, lived in the rectories.

Nonetheless, a valiant effort was undertaken to seek a monastic style of life. In fact, a phenomenal increase of vocations brought about such large numbers that a novitiate wing had to be built. At its height there were ninety men in formation. Father John Neitzel was the Master of Professed and I was the Master of Novices. Priority was given to a proper celebration of the Liturgy of the Hours and the daily celebration of the Eucharist in the Mass. We were influenced by the new liturgical movement in the Church as well as the traditions of our European Abbeys.

Theological training became the full time commitment of the students. No longer did they teach two classes a day at our high school. A number of our men had just returned from Rome with doctorates in the various theological disciplines. Outside professors were hired to travel weekly to the Abbey to teach the scripture courses. A summer house was rented in Milwaukee so that our theology students could begin graduate work at Marquette to prepare for their teaching specialties. Seminary discipline was not much different from that at the old Abbey.

Most novices were eighteen year-olds. At vesting in the religious habit, each novice was given a new first name. The first year novice was cloistered, that is, required to remain on campus except for medical reasons.

The second-year novice could begin or continue college studies and received their first one-week vacation home at the end of that year. A spirit of silence was expected during the day in all parts of the Abbey except for recreation times after lunch and dinner. A *magnum silentium* (great silence) was practiced from 9:00 p.m. until after breakfast the following morning. Families could visit the seminarians once a month on Sunday afternoon. Fraternization between novices and professed and between all of them and priests was limited. The novices wore habits at all times except for work, play, and sleep. The students wore black suits, black socks, black shoes, white shirts, and black ties when traveling outside the Abbey.

The community lined up in the cloister walks prior to liturgical prayer as well as for meals and entered the church and dining room in a procession. The members sat at table according to age, from the oldest at the head of the table to the youngest at the end. Most meals were eaten in silence while a seminarian read from the Rule of Augustine and other books. Students were expected to meet with their formation director or his assistant once a month. Confessors were assigned, but the students could request an alternative. Alcohol was served rarely. Occasionally a film was shown. Novices did the sacristy work, took their turn at serving at table, cleaned their residence area, and washed the windows in the cloister walks and church entrance.

Four afternoons, they worked outside on the grounds, weather permitting. All novices were expected to read books about prayer and lives of saints for at least thirty minutes a day. The first-year men attended a one-hour class conducted by the novice master Monday through Friday.

From 1959 to 1966 (the last year of the Second Vatican Council) the number of candidates for the novitiate increased each year. In 1966 almost every room for novices and professed was occupied.

During my years as novice master, I supervised the various aspects of their lives as described above. Having lived most of these norms during my own years as a novice, I was familiar with the system and generally understood what was needed. Of course, I had to learn the increased ritual rules for solemn Masses as well as the Liturgy of the Hours choral office. In my years as director of novices, I found them responsive to our rules and customs, and we generally got along well.

Only once did I overreact to a breach of discipline. On Good Friday afternoon, after the lengthy services, I noticed that a few of the men had gathered at the entrance of the property, about a half-mile from the Abbey door, and were both breaking the silence required on Good Friday, and also the rule about contact with outsiders. I rounded them up and, I'm sorry to say, delivered a rant that I prefer to forget. Some of the survivors of that class who are now veteran priests seldom fail to remind me of my behavior that day. They are good natured and I laugh about it with them.

Working with the novices was a form of continual spiritual renewal of my own life. By reviewing the basics of religious life I naturally found myself measuring my own observance and forced to constantly evaluate my own commitment to Christ in the life of a Norbertine. By taking them through each liturgical year I drew their attention, and mine, too, to the prayer life of the Church. I shared my love of scripture with them and benefitted from the new commentaries being published. I introduced them to the new scripture "stars" such as Passionist Father Barnabas Ahern and Sulpician Father Raymond Brown.

Father Ahern witnessed a deep personal spiritual life and was, for me, another St. Paul. Father Brown was a master teacher who combined faith and scholarship to produce lucid and inspiring commentaries, especially his masterpiece volumes on St. John's Gospel. Their enlightening commentaries—many of which were published by St. John's Abbey Press—gave new life and accessibility to the Bible.

The predominant daily presence of the liturgy and the other ceremonies performed with care and reverence, were unbeatable sources of training in prayer. Seeing our choir stalls, seating ninety Norbertines, filling up with young men served as a witness of faith and a promise of a vibrant future for our community. Sadly this was not to be, but that is another story. Because of the growing number of seminarians, our Sunday Mass attendance outgrew our pews in the nave so we put up folding chairs in both of our side chapels to handle the crowd. A great many of these people were families of the seminarians who came to worship with their sons.

Since the formation program is a statement of what the Abbey community thinks about itself and its mission, formation inevitably reflects this vision at a given time. Continuing discussions and clarification of what the vows of poverty, chastity, and obedience mean, what apostolates are suitable, what is the relationship between prayer life and ministry affect what is most desirable for formation.

Issues undreamed of in 1959, when the new Abbey opened, would slowly begin to affect Abbey living and formation in the years leading up to Vatican II, more so in the years that followed.

CHAPTER EIGHT

Lumen Vitae

The Church's Teaching Mission Explored

The whole of Christ's life was a continual teaching: His silences, His miracles, His gestures, His prayer, His love for people, His special affection for the little and the poor, His acceptance of the total sacrifice on the Cross for the redemption of the world and his resurrection are the actualization of his word and the fulfillment of his revelation.

—*On Catechesis in Our Time*, Pope John Paul II, p.9

AT the end of my fourth year as novice master I was surprised by one of the recommendations of our Abbot General who had just completed a visitation, or evaluation, of our community. He told Abbot Killeen, "Father McBride needs more training." Abbot Killeen summoned me to his office and broke the news to me, adding that I would be sent to Rome for a year for further training for a year. In the course of our conversation I mentioned my interest in the Lumen Vitae (Light of Life) catechetical institute in Brussels, Belgium. It was probably the teacher in me that attracted me to this possibility. I pointed out how my morning classes were largely devoted to teaching scripture, liturgy, and a spirituality related to these topics. The abbot maintained that Rome would be the best place for me to study, but invited me to look deeper into the details of Lumen Vitae.

As providence would have it, the next issue of St. John's Benedictine Abbey magazine, *Worship*, contained an article on Lumen Vitae written by a Father Marx who had just taken the course. His piece offered many details on the institute and ended with a positive judgment on the experience. The institute, sponsored by the Jesuit Fathers, began at Louvain University as a center for scholarly research on catechesis. They envisioned a nine-month year for a student body of 150 male and female students made up of laity, priests, nuns, and brothers. They would limit enrollment of seven students each from Europe, Canada, and the United States. The remainder of the students would come from Africa, Asia, and South America. This was to ensure that the institute maintained a missionary priority. Students were also expected to be able to pass on what they had learned to others. To that end, teaching "field trips" to parishes, schools, and universities rounded out the course requirements.

I presented all this to Abbot Killeen who looked interested but reminded me that he needed to consult the Council and others before making a decision. By June of 1962, it was decided that I could apply for enrollment.

Lectures at Lumen Vitae would generally be delivered

in French, supplemented with ear phone translations and outlines of the talks in the major languages. To prepare for this, I attended a French course for beginners at our college and also met once a week with a French speaking woman in Green Bay for basic conversation.

The Abbot appointed Father Finnegan as temporary novice master while I was away. He was and is a conscientious Norbertine, and just right for the task. The last week in August 1963, I flew to Brussels where I was met by two American Sisters of Loreto who gave me a cheerful welcome and brought me to my home away from home, the Pension Suisse, a comfortable townhouse located two blocks from the classroom building.

All of September was devoted to immersion in French. I had a small tape recorder with which I recorded the evening news and listened to it over and over until I began to hear what was being said. I also brought with me several workbooks. One of our priests back at the Abbey, Father Louis Defnet, gave me the phone numbers and addresses of two Belgian families who were relatives of his. I did get in touch with them and periodically visited with them. One of the families had a number of small children who loved to teach me French. They were quick to correct me and always laughing.

I quickly made friends with a young Irish priest from Dublin, Leo Close, who was training to do missionary work in Dunedin, New Zealand. He was a big man, six feet tall, 180 pounds. His legs were paralyzed. In the summer before his last year in the All Hallows Seminary, which prepared the men for priestly service in mission countries, he went on a hiking trip to Europe, and during a hike in the mountains he slipped and broke his back. He lost the use of his legs but learned how to drive and do minimal movement with crutches. He visited Rome and was able to meet with Pope John XXIII. He asked for permission to be ordained and received it. He showed me the rosary Pope John gave him. He had a great sense of humor and excelled in storytelling. Another Irish priest, Father O'Donnell, came with him for the course and helped him celebrate Mass among other tasks. Leo joined the local Irish Club and enrolled me as a member as well. The members loved to sing the old melodies and dance and play cards and trade the news from back home.

Leo introduced me to the films of the Swedish Ingmar Bergman, such as *The Virgin Spring* and *The Seventh Seal*. I was puzzled by the films, so dark and slow, so unlike Hollywood, but definitely a favorite of the critics. The theater where we saw the films was on the second floor and had no elevator, and so I was tasked with holding onto Leo's wheel chair for the ascent and descent. The trip down the stairs worried me most. I visualized him slipping away from me. Thank God, that never happened, mainly due to his firm grip on the wheels.

Our classes began the first week of October. Lumen Vitae was housed in a former mansion. The ballroom had been transformed into a lecture hall. During that first month, the morning lecturers were guest speakers who were *periti*, that is theological experts who accompanied their bishops to the Second Vatican Council, which had just opened. This was an unexpected premium: a first-hand crash course on the issues being discussed in Vatican II.

In the afternoons that first month we began courses on scripture, psychology, and anthropology. I soon realized the catechetical nature of all the courses. We were being taught what and how to teach our religion in the light of recent studies of our traditional subjects and the contributions of the social sciences as resources. I was familiar with the liturgical and scriptural movements in America and found an enrichment of these topics through discussions of God's plan to save us, the role of salvation history, life in Christ through the celebration of the liturgy, and the need for evangelizing ourselves and those we serve.

The teachers were mostly excellent. I remember in a special way the Redemptorist Father Bernard Haring whose book, *The Law of Love*, was a bestseller in the United States. He had a gentle and humble, yet persuasive, teaching style. He had a way of approaching morality from the viewpoint of love and happiness. He said that true happiness, following the Beatitudes, is the best motivator for being moral. God has planted in us a natural desire to be happy, and God alone will satisfy us. This was not a new concept. Augustine, for instance, wrote,

> How is it then that I seek you, Lord? Since in
> seeking you, my God, I seek a happy life, let me

seek you so that my soul may live, for my body
draws life from my soul, and my soul draws life
from you.

(St. Augustine, Confessions, 10, 20)

But, Father Haring had a way of conveying these eter-
nal truths in a way that was fresh and enlightening.

As I listened to Haring, I thought it was unfortunate
that many believe that Catholic moral teachings make us
unhappy. In fact, I think a part of me believed that too. I
had mentioned earlier that Father Albin tried to teach me
otherwise, but a legalistic morality stuck with me. The
restrictions of the laws and commandments limit what I
can do, I thought. Yet I have read the opening lines of the
Sermon on the Mount with the eight beatitudes countless
times. I heard the word beatitude but somehow it didn't
register as joy. And the roads to joy don't sound like the
happy life. "Blessed [happy] are you when they insult you
and persecute you and utter every kind of evil against
you [falsely] because of me." (Mt 5:11) In a way, Christ's
words, improperly understood, could sound like eight
paths to misery.

Haring was aware of this objection and the error
which drove so many people away from God. He said
we cannot dwell on happiness alone. He emphasized the
intrinsic union of happiness with Christ's laws of love of
God and neighbor. Unless we have a love relationship
with God and all people, we will never grasp the true
meaning of Christ's challenges. Haring unpacked the

lengthy teachings about the covenant in the Bible: from the rainbow that wedded heaven and earth for Noah, to the call of Abraham and the dream of a posterity as fruitful as the stars of heaven and the sands by sea, to the meeting of Moses with God at Sinai who insisted on a covenant love relationship before giving the commandments, to, finally, the greatest evidence of the covenant: the arrival of the Word made flesh in the marvel of the incarnation.

The covenant was completed with the most profound example of sacrificial love that ever happened, the lesson that Jesus gave us at the Cross. Haring had a way of dramatizing the secret of the covenant as a relationship rooted in love which is a gift from God and a necessary prelude to happiness. I saw this as a creative catechetical tool for presenting Catholic morality to our students.

While I was inspired by Haring, I didn't realize how soon the roles of love and happiness would face unexpected false interpretations of the true meaning of love. Situation ethics treated love as merely a form of selfishness. The rise of the sexual revolution obscured the authentic understanding of love and perverted it into simple lust. It was a formula that, sadly, undermined marriage and family. In the years that followed, the role of love took hold of our moral compass. But it wasn't real love. The culture that arose had lost the sense of sin, which reduced love to sheer sentimentality and lust. It is necessary to view love, even with the best of ideals, in the light of faith and the Church's traditions.

It was a bleak time in many respects, but the future
brought extraordinary leaders for the Church such as
Pope Paul VI, whose courage in publishing *Humanae
Vitae* was an outstanding support for our moral lives.
Following him was the historic papacies of Pope John
Paul II and his successor, Benedict XVI. These lights,
shining through the morass of modern culture, assure us
that God is still present to our world. As a catechist, I
treasure the new Catechism which is a sure guide to our
doctrinal and moral teachings. I did not know all that
as I finished my days at Lumen Vitae. As you will see, I
strayed for a time and lived to regret it.

* * *   * * *   * * *

As the weeks and months went by, I began to see Lumen
Vitae's vision of teaching religion (catechesis). I saw that I
was being called to teach God's message, which is his plan
to save us from sin and evil and to transform us by union
with his Son who wins the graces we need and the gift of
the Spirit who brings us a life of holiness. I was invited to
explore the four sources of God's desires for us: scripture,
liturgy, doctrine, witness. I would communicate these
four treasures by teaching, worshiping, studying, and
showing others its effects in my life. Our teachers treated
these sources from the viewpoint of attitudes and habits
which guide us to ensure that the church's inheritance of
God's revelation will be preserved and adequately taught
and preached.

In union with Christ, I would try to call my students

and listeners to a faith journey and lifelong trust in the loving God that comes to meet them. Lumen Vitae, therefore, was teaching much more than classroom formality or pulpit proclamation: it taught a person-to-person event, communicated in freedom and respecting the freedom of the listener.

In another vein, I wish to recall two other events during my year at Lumen Vitae. Father Close drove me to the Benedictine Abbey of Maredsous in southern Belgium, where we visited the grave of Abbot Marmion, in the vault of the abbots beneath the church. I recalled Marmion's influence on me in seminary days and thanked him.

At the end of our year, Father Leo told us that he was flying to Dunedin, New Zealand for his mission. Later I learned he became a popular radio priest whose programs supported the faith of Catholics and others to join the Church. I regret to report his ministry lasted only ten years before he died of cancer. May God be good to him.

Easter Break: Holy Week in the Holy Land

> We adore you, O Christ, and we praise you,
> for by your holy Cross you have redeemed the
> world.
>
> On the third day, you rose again,
> glorious in majesty to reign.
> O let us swell the joyful strain.
> Alleluia!

We were given a three-week break in the spring, during which I was able to make a trip to the Holy Land. My first stop was in Rome where my Norbertine priest friend, Father Roman Vanasse met me and brought me to the Norbertine Generalate. The day I arrived, Father Roman took me to St. Peter's where Pope John XXIII was meeting with several thousand people from Sotto il Monte, his birth place. He looked and sounded lively, though he was fatally ill and destined to die in three months. He loved seeing his people, mostly farmers from his home town, and it clearly enlivened him that day.

Father Roman translated Pope John's words for me:

> I know many of you work the farms. At night
> you come home, tired, with an ache in your back.
> When you enter and close the door you can see
> the crucifix over it. Now in the bedroom of my
> apartment , when I wake up in the morning, I
> see the crucifix over my door. Each morning I
> look at Jesus and say, "They did it to you. They
> will do it to me. So what's the complaining?"

All these years later, I still find that anecdote compelling and it moves me to repeat his prayer while gazing at the crucifix.

Father Roman and I spent the next five days at a convent guest house on the Isle of Capri. We had long talks about the future of our community. I said, "We need a thrust to greatness." I am not sure I really knew what I was talking about, but I never forgot it. It was hardly a humble thought as Roman reminded me. I will probably be chasing humility until my last proud breath

To get to the Holy Land inexpensively I flew with a group of elderly Italian women led by two Franciscan Friars. Also with me were my Lumen Vitae classmates, Jesuit Father Mark Link and an English missionary to Africa, Adrian Smith. Father Link would later acquire a national reputation in the States as a lecturer and writer of high school religion textbooks and a series of daily meditations on the liturgy.

We flew first to Cairo and then to Jerusalem, arriving on Palm Sunday. After settling in at the Franciscan guest house, we drove to the peak of the Mount of Olives where we joined a crowd of pilgrims. The Latin Patriarch greeted us and then chanted, "*Lauda Jerusalem, Dominum, Lauda deum, tuuum Sion.*" (Praise the Lord, Jerusalem. Praise your God, O Sion.) We all received large olive branches and walked in procession down the Mount of Olives to St. Stephen's, the entry to the Temple area. I was told that five thousand pilgrims marched with us, singing hymns from their homelands. Lined on each side of us were throngs of Muslim families watching our parade with their children holding balloons and eating ice cream. I was reminded of the old saying, "Everyone loves a parade." We attended Benediction of the Blessed Sacrament in the plaza in front of St. Anne's church inside the city. As the patriarch raised the monstrance to bless us, we raised our olive branches and waved them as the choir sang, "Hosannah to the Son of David."

In the subsequent days we visited the church of the Transfiguration and the remains of the Capernaum synagogue, in front of which Jesus had taught a crowd the meaning of the Eucharist. We also could see the Lake of Galilee, where Jesus walked on the water and, later, preached from a boat when the crowd on shore was too big. We saw where the house of Jesus, Mary, and Joseph might have been in Nazareth. On Holy Thursday, we concelebrated a Mass in a chapel overlooking Jerusalem. On Good Friday morning we walked the *Via Dolorosa*, Christ's Way of the Cross, with a multitude of Christians. That afternoon we toured the church that was built over Calvary and the shrine of the Resurrection.

On Holy Saturday morning we entered the Jewish side of the city. In those days the Palestinian and Jewish quarters were separated by a barbed wire wall, with machine gun nests perched at various checkpoints. We saw the Upper Room and a jail cell in hole in the ground with a manhole cover where Jesus may have been imprisoned after his arrest. There is a sign there with Isaiah, Chapter 53: "He was pierced for our offenses and crushed for our sins. Upon him was the chastisement that made us whole. By his stripes, we were healed." (Is 53:5)

On Holy Saturday night we participated in the Easter Vigil at the convent of the Sisters of Zion, a community of nuns, women who converted to the Church from Judaism. It is built over a stone pavement dating from Christ's time and thought to be the site of the pillar where the Roman soldiers scourged Jesus and crowned him with thorns. The historic setting made our identity with Christ more vivid both in his Passion and his victory over death in his Resurrection.

After the liturgy, I asked my companions to go ahead without me. I wanted to walk alone that night where I could see the large Passover moon and try to absorb the many impressions of the Gospels I had received that past week. I let my mind wander back two thousand years to the days of the first celebrations of the Eucharist. Possibly, a number of those who participated had also celebrated the Breaking of the Bread in the Upper Room where Jesus instituted the Eucharist. I let my imagination collapse between them and me. About this hour they would have finished their liturgies, just as I did. Their last song would have been shouts of joy from their roof tops as they sang: "Come, Lord Jesus!"

I heard Jesus sing back, "Yes, I am coming soon!" (Rev 22:20)

Reflection on Lumen Vitae

One of the great gifts of the Lumen Vitae program was the missionary zeal for teaching the truths of Christ as mediated by the Church. The majority presence of students from Africa and Latin America expanded our awareness of a world Church, and their enthusiasm for the Church inspired us to have a fresh point of view about our faith. Their fervor and that of the faculty was contagious. It fired me up and I sensed this was true of the other twenty students from Canada, Europe, and the United States. The genius of Lumen Vitae may be that it communicated new perspectives about scripture, liturgy, doctrine, and witness in way that wove tradition and renewal with a generous heart.

The program was penetrated with joy at new possibilities for teaching a faith that was ever ancient and ever new. The program took seriously the presentation of the Gospel as "good news." At the same time it was not unaware of the presence of evil. Still, there was a joyful tone, because the good news said that "Christ has risen," and that evil will never prevail in long run. I felt that I was being trained in a faith-based optimism that never avoided admitting the curse of evil, but never forgot the full message of Christ's death and resurrection. Long before our current and welcome goal of the New Evangelization, the seeds of this vision already existed at Lumen Vitae.

I am grateful to the staff at Lumen Vitae for the enthusiasm for teaching religion they communicated to me. I thank them for their guidance in ways to be a catechist. They did not just impart knowledge about the faith, but they showed me how to teach it, how to witness it, and how to help others to live what Jesus and the Church are all about. It was a game changer for me. Near the end of May, I finished my studies and returned home, where I resumed my responsibilities with the novices.

CHAPTER NINE

After Lumen Vitae

Let our members raise their hearts to heavenly
things, not seeking the vanities of the world.

—Rule of Saint Augustine

COMMENTING on the Rule of St. Augustine in his
book, *It Is Like a Mirror*, Norbertine Brother Frank
Kazenbroot wrote,

> What does Augustine mean by this sentence?
> We need to yearn with all our hearts for that
> higher life with God, that life that the scripture
> identifies as the kingdom of God. According to
> Augustine, our earthly appearance is a life that is
> transitory with its fame, glamour and riches. In a
> religious community this earthly glory is no lon-
> ger sought. What really counts is the kingdom of
> God, the land of peace, love and justice.

(Brother Frank Kazenbroot,
It Is Like a Mirror—Reflections on the Rule of St. Augustine,
Alt Publishing Co., De Pere, WI, 22)

I was energized by my year at Lumen Vitae and proceeded with the vision I described earlier as an approach

that would help the novices with the basics of religious life. They still needed the first months to get used to the schedule, the way to participate in the Liturgy of the Hours, and chanting in Latin. They had to learn Gregorian chant for the Masses and the many details of community that I described already. They brought their first fervor with them and appeared open to our demands. I met with each of them monthly with the hope of having a more personal relationship with them and helping them with difficulties that emerged. I also developed some extra programs.

I gradually judged that a monthly group meeting with the second-year men was needed to monitor both their college classes and their spiritual progress. I had an excellent assistant, Father Bernard Brunette, who was a science teacher and familiar with secondary school students. The questioning of basics—Why the vow of celibacy? Why "blind" obedience? Why discourage secular reading?—was beginning to appear, but was not yet troublesome.

I met with the first-year men each morning from Monday to Friday, giving a lecture on various topics, including the life of St. Norbert, the history of the Order, the vows, and the Rule of St. Augustine. I also developed talks on the Gospels, the liturgy, and spirituality. At the time I was impressed by *This Tremendous Lover*, a book by the Irish Trappist, Father Eugene Boylan. He presented the Gospel accounts of Christ's teachings and witness of the virtue of love so vividly that I felt the energy of Jesus flowing from his pages. I passed on my enthusiasm for Boylan so fervently that one day the novices appeared with paper tabs affixed to their habits with the title, "This Tremendous Lover" and gave me my own copy that claimed, "THE Trememdous Lover."

I also had them study the reflections on the Liturgy by Canon Pius Parsch. He was a member of the community of Canons Regular at Klosterneuberg in Vienna. He had a talent for linking the daily liturgy to our prayer lives. Side by side with Parsch, I also provided the novices with excellent booklets on the meaning and background of the Gospels, published by St. John's Abbey in Collegeville, MN, particularly those by Fathers Brown and Ahern. It seemed to me that consistent study of the liturgy and scripture were a proper counterpart to our daily prayer life. We attempted to live what we studied and study what we hoped to live with fervor and faith.

My training at Lumen Vitae inspired me to begin reaching out beyond our community. I developed the idea of a series of lectures on the lessons of catechesis I learned at Lumen Vitae for the Sisters in the Green Bay area. I proposed the idea to a Bay Settlement Franciscan, Sister Jude, who held the office of religious education in the diocese. She liked the idea and began working on the permissions and details to make it happen. The following spring, I began the first evening talk in St. Mary of the Angels' church hall for an audience of about one hundred sisters. We met for nine more weeks. Their response was positive, and I received a request to do the same for the sisters in the Appleton area, with similar results.

One of the best blessings that arose during my lecture series came to me in the person of Patricia Rupp,
who came to all our meetings. She and her husband
Bob and their three children became good friends. Over
the years I had made friendships with families, but the
Rupps and I became closer. Patricia invited me to their
home. Bob was in charge of the Green Bay office of the
Neilson Company and at the time he was overseeing the
completion of their new office building. Their children,
Catherine, Robert, and Mary, were in elementary school
at the time. I watched them grow, marry, have children,
and settle into family life. Their Catholic faith has never
faltered in all the years I have known them, and I continue to celebrate their friendship with a gratitude that is
boundless.

In the meantime, Pastor Roger Bourland of the
Methodist church in Green Bay came to see me with a
proposal. He was well known locally for his pastoral outreach to the Green Bay Packers' Protestant players. He
said that given the interest in ecumenism stirred by the
Council, it would be a good idea to co-teach Paul's Letter
to the Ephesians once a week for eight weeks. He had
obtained permission to use the dining room of Prange's
department store, which would also provide free rolls
and coffee. He proposed we call the program, "Bible and
Brunch." Roger said that he would give the first lecture
and I would field the questions. The following week, I
would give the talk and he would take the questions. I

received permission from both the abbot and the bishop. Roger and I worked well together, and the sessions were popular, drawing a full house each week.

The head of our theology department, Father Benjamin Mackin, asked me if I would be willing to teach a class in preaching for the fourth-year men. I had long been interested in the process of preaching and was happy to accept. After a year of working with them, I was not satisfied with the results. Predictably, they were not at ease preaching to each other. Some of them took refuge in giving summaries of doctrinal topics from systematic theology or the moral theology course. A few of them found it hard to open with a story. Several were too hard in evaluating the others. I developed an alternative plan. I met with five couples who were friends of mine and asked them if they would be willing to gather a group of their friends every two weeks and listen to my students preach. They agreed. I called it, "A "Living Room Homily."

The students were required to deliver an eight- to ten-minute homily without notes. They were to begin with a story that illustrated the Gospel message. They were to make only one point. Not only did the students like this, but the laity enjoyed taking a role in training future preachers. Years later, my students repeatedly said what a success that was. I received feedback from the couples as well as from the students. They became more aware of laity response. I oversaw this program for two years, and was planning refinements, when I was engaged in another apostolate.

Had I stayed at the Abbey, I would have had some follow-up preaching classes so I could see how well they had grown in preaching skills. In retrospect, I would not use this approach as the sole form of preacher training. I believe regular classroom training is essential, so long as it is implemented with pastoral parish experience and perhaps some experience with "Living Room Homilies."

Before proceeding to the next step in my faith journey, I need to praise Abbot Killeen, my spiritual father during my years as a novice master at the new Abbey. He was a strong but gentle father, who provided an Abbey way of life with the daily splendor of the Eucharist and a growing tradition of the Liturgy of the Hours that was more in harmony with the great Abbeys of Europe. Despite its newness for all of us, Abbot Killeen was a patient and loving leader, who walked with and encouraged us. He followed my efforts in training the novices with interest, refining my approach and offering ways to enrich the formation of our new men. I could never have progressed without him and the participation of all the members of the Abbey in a community commitment.

CHAPTER TEN

How I Became a Published Writer

> Jeremiah, write all the words I have spoken to
> you in a book.
>
> —Jeremiah 30:2

> Let not loyalty and faithfulness forsake you.
> Write them on the tablet of your heart.
>
> —Proverbs 3:3

S CRIPTURE, especially the Old Testament, often refers to writers and the prophets being inspired by God with messages of infinite importance for his people. Gentle reader, by now you know that has not been my experience. I will say that, as I moved along, I felt the need to implore Christ and Mary for words and ideas. Gratefully, I may say, they have been generous with encouragement and sparking my creativity, though I cannot attribute my faltering text to inspiration from on high. At any rate, here is the story of the birth of a writer.

From time to time, I felt the urge to write and submit an article based on my biblical preaching to a magazine. I received a number of rejection slips from prominent secular publishers such as the *Saturday Evening Post* and

Parade magazine. Bible stories were not their specialty. I should have sought advisors, who would, undoubtedly, have told me to submit, instead, to Catholic publications. Instead, I overreached. After a while, I concluded that God did not want me to be a published writer.

But God had other plans. The abbot asked me to help Father Jafolla with the weekend retreats for the students from our high school in Green Bay. I asked permission to attend a weekend youth retreat run by the Dominican Fathers in Chicago so I could get some idea of the topics and the procedures. During a break, I was sitting quietly in my guest room and noticed a typewriter. I sat before it and began writing about the Psalms as songs of prayer. Busily, I put my thoughts on paper until I had completed five double-spaced pages. I mailed it to *Worship* magazine, published by the Benedictines in Minnesota, and they accepted it.

A few months after its publication, I received a letter from Bruce publishers in Milwaukee. They invited me to meet with them to discuss my interest in revising Cleveland's Bishop Elwell's popular high school religion series. They told me they had seen my article in *Worship* and noted that I had studied at Lumen Vitae. I made an appointment and drove down to meet with the editors. Tucked in my coat pocket were the outlines of my lectures to the Sisters in Wisconsin in case there would be time to discuss that.

For two hours we discussed their proposal. I finally said that I believed that my approach would not work.

Then I made a counter proposal to write a catechetical work along the lines of my lecture series, but they were not interested. On my way out of the office, a staff member came out of his room and said to me, "Father, do you have any homilies for the new liturgy?"

What was new? By our standards, the only change in the liturgical texts then was reading the epistle and Gospel in English, not in Latin and English, and the priest turning to face the people. The other difference was, that in preaching, we had the rich insights of the first approved document by Vatican II: The Constitution the Sacred Liturgy. I had already returned to Sunday radio preaching at the new Abbey. I had a typed copy of almost all of them which I used, not to preach from, but to send copies for those who requested them. The result was my first book, *Homilies for the New Liturgy*. A year later, Bruce publishers sent me a contract for a second book that would be entitled, *Catechetics: A Theology of Proclamation*. These first adventures in book publishing would expand with my more than twenty-year association with Our Sunday Visitor Publishers and St. Anthony Messenger Publishers (now known as Franciscan Media).

Another book opportunity followed soon thereafter. Sisters Johnice Cohan and Elizabeth Fowkes, members of the Immaculate Heart of Mary community in Monroe, Michigan, were interested in my Lumen Vitae background and they invited me to their residence for a weekend to discuss catechetical issues. They had opened a popular summer program on catechesis, accredited by

the Jesuit University of Detroit. They invited me to be
a presenter for a one-week series. Eventually this led to
my involvement in their elementary school religion textbooks, entitled *Bible, Life and Worship*. They had gone
to France to meet with the priest author of the texts for
the first four grades. They obtained rights to publish an
English edition in the United States through the Allyn
and Bacon Company in Boston.

By this time they had written the fifth- to sev-
enth-grade texts and asked me to consider writing the
eighth-grade text on Church history. They suggested I
come to Detroit the next summer and spend a week writing the first three chapters. When I arrived the following
summer, they said, "Go up to the attic and begin writing and then show us what you have done." I had already
been thinking and reading about possible topics to start
the history. My style was straight narrative: "This happened." "That occurred." "Then the effect was . . ." When
I showed it to them, they scanned the material and then
slowly tore up the pages. "Go back upstairs and write a
story approach. Our students would never get into this."

Chastened, I started over. To my surprise I liked
doing a fictional account of what happened in a way
that taught the truth of the experience. I started with
Pentecost, quoting a few lines from Peter's sermon. I created four imaginary characters in the crowd discussing
his thoughts and what they could mean. For the second
lesson, I imagined St. Paul as a journalist answering pastoral problems. Here is sample:

Q. I am a Christian homemaker and I am concerned about the contaminated meat (meat previously offered to idols) that I find at the meat counter. Can I in good conscience buy such meat for my family?

A. Don't worry, the meat really isn't contaminated because the gods in question do not really exist. Still, if you think you would scandalize a fellow Christian by buying and eating it, you might for that person's sake, pass it up. (Read 1 Cor 8:1–13)

They approved this approach, which I followed up with the Reformation, gradually introducing more and more documented history. From then on, I wrote in the traditional manner but stressing the lives of the saints and outstanding Catholics such as Dorothy Day and Thomas Merton to give history a more personal and inspiring tone. The original edition was published in four large-sized, illustrated booklets.

My editor at Allyn and Bacon was Bob Hope, predictably teased for his name, but no pushover. His standards were high and uncompromising. I learned a great deal about effective writing from Bob, God bless him. The text enjoyed a great run from 1970 to 1978. The series eventually went out of print due to health problems of the two Sisters and their departure from their community. Thanks to St. Anthony Messenger, the text was reborn in one-volume form in 1980. They published a third edition in 2009 that includes the papacy of John Paul II and the life of Mother Teresa of Calcutta and similar contemporary references.

CHAPTER ELEVEN

Catholic University

The Privilege of Forming Future Catechetical Leaders

Before I formed you in the womb, I knew you,
and before you were born, I consecrated you.
and appointed you to be a prophet to the nations.

—Jeremiah 1:5

A T the same time that I was beginning my relationship with Sisters Johnice and Elizabeth, I received a letter from Father Gerald Sloyan, inviting me to be a visiting professor in the Religious Education department at Catholic University in Washington, DC He had read and liked my book on catechesis and had also noted my Lumen Vitae studies

I brought the letter to Abbot Killeen, who, eventually, gave me permission. I arrived at the campus in mid-August of 1966 and found my quarters in Caldwell hall, primarily a residence for priest students. I lived on the floor set aside for professors. My quarters included a study, a bedroom, and bath. The building had a chapel and a dining room for the residents and some classrooms on the first floor. The first priest I met there was Father Dan

Maguire, a priest of the archdiocese of Philadelphia, who would be teaching morality. Friendly and witty, he was an amiable companion. Sadly, he would one day marry and leave the priesthood and become a major dissenter from Catholic teachings.

He seemed to know the neighborhood and suggested we go to a restaurant for dinner, since none was yet served at Caldwell. After dinner we roamed the campus as he pointed out the main buildings. I noted the National Shrine of the Immaculate Conception towering over the campus. The structure was completed. Over the years, the mosaics and other art works would be added. In recent years, the annual Pro-Life Mass is held there. Once classes began, I met many of the priest students for graduate degrees, especially Canon Law, in the dining room at Caldwell.

I was happy to see one of my Norbertine brothers, Father Kevin Grognet, who was completing his graduate degree in clinical psychology. He had a car which he generously shared with me. He introduced me to two professors who were born and raised in Green Bay, Jim and Dick Youniss. They came from a Lebanese family in Green Bay. Jim taught developmental psychology with an emphasis on children's learning stages in the light of Piaget's studies. Dick taught clinical psychology and was a productive artist. Jim and his wife Dorothy were a young couple, then raising four children. They welcomed me into their family circle and during my twenty years in Washington, we met many times, especially for

Thanksgiving. Dorothy had learned to cook Lebanese cuisine and taught me to appreciate it. They were then, and remain now, models of a devoted family and enduring kindness to friends. I am grateful beyond words.

I owe Kevin another debt. Before my second Christmas in Washington, Kevin invited me to drive with him to Clearwater, Florida, for a brief vacation with the Tobias family—Jim and Shirley and their children, Michelle, Jamie, Lori, and Greg. They had a large rambling house near the "king of beaches," an impossibly wide stretch of the whitest sand that never seems to stop. Over the years, the Tobias family graciously invited me back, and I was able to make it for two holidays.

* * *   * * *   * * *

As I look back at the title of this section, I wonder about the expression of "my forming" future catechists. The idea seems to encroach on God's territory, as in the case of Jeremiah's pre-born life. On the other hand, if I think of myself as an instrument of God in the education and formation of future catechetical leaders, then I can live with it, as in fact I am doing. Religious educators need to be idealistic because the care of souls and minds has consequences beyond sharing ideas. The Jeremiah quote matches "I knew you" with "I consecrated you." Knowing has the feeling of exterior contact. Consecrating has the sense of personal involvement in the holiness and destiny of the student. All the more, then, must I be an instrument of God's work. So let it be said. So let it be done.

The Professor

> Go, therefore, make disciples of all nations . . .
> teaching them to observe all that I have com-
> manded you. And behold, I am with you always,
> until the end of the age.
>
> —Mt 28:19–20

My responsibilities included teaching two courses, one each semester, for the graduate students. I received approval to develop a course on the "History of Catechesis," for the first semester and a course on the "Human Dimension of Catechesis" for the second semester. There were thirty-five students in the classes. Priests, brothers, sisters, and laity made up the student body, all destined to be teachers or directors of religious education in parishes or to prepare for posts in diocesan religious education leadership roles.

I also was asked to teach two courses each semester to undergraduate students, one for Catholic students and the other for non-Catholics. The latter were required, as were all students at the university, to take four religion courses. For the Catholic students I developed a survey of the Old Testament for the first semester and a survey of the New Testament for the second semester. The religious education department entitled the courses for non-Catholics "Judaeo-Christian Studies." These courses covered scripture and writings of Jewish and Protestant leaders such as Rabbi Abraham Heschel and C. S. Lewis.

The tone was meant to be ecumenical and respectful to the variety of faith persuasions in the classes. I would also include Catholic teachings in areas where we differed from other faiths

In my second year teaching this course, a student named Ivan joined us. He was raised in Communist Russia and never raised in the faith. While a sailor in the Soviet navy, he jumped ship while docked in Southampton, England. He sought asylum, which was granted, and eventually came to America and obtained a scholarship to our university. He looked the part of a Russian; big build, Slavic face, a gentle giant. There was an elderly European priest in Caldwell doing research at the university. He spoke Russian. I asked him if he would be willing to meet with Ivan and help him to understand the texts in the Old Testament that I would assign him. I also purchased a Russian language Bible for Ivan.

I required Ivan to attend our classes and to consider meeting with the priest as part of his homework. I met with Ivan each week to check on his progress. After five weeks, I was disappointed to hear him say, "I knew that God did not like Jews." I discovered it was an opinion derived from the mentor I had engaged to help him. It was also, partly, due to his own Russian background. I canceled the arrangement with the mentor. I explained that we are opposed to anti-Semitism and we may not cite scripture to support it. At the end of the course, I asked him to draw a picture of what he learned about God and his Son, Jesus. He drew a cross, framed it with hearts and wrote the word Love several times around it. He did not return for the next semester and I never saw him again, but wondered how he made out in the following years.

* * *   * * *   * * *

In the Autumn of 1965, the Fathers of Vatican II were finishing their meetings, and the issues they had raised attracted widespread interest. The *New Yorker* published "Letters from Vatican II," written by Xavier Rynne, (the pseudonym of Father Francis X. Murphy). He established the story line of the Council as a battle between backward conservatives and enlightened liberals. He tied his interpretation exclusively to *aggiornamento*, translated as "updating," and the media followed his vision of the Council. The trouble with that judgment was that it fostered popular inattention to another essential movement of the times, mainly developed by French thinkers such as Congar and DeLubac. Their theme was *ressourcement*, a rediscovery of the riches of the Church's two-thousand-year treasury, a return to the very headwaters of the Christian tradition, especially the Fathers of the Church. Frankly, I, too, was unaware of this at the time. It was my loss.

Often it was difficult to judge which opinions were faithful to the Council and which ones were not. In any case, I could anticipate questions from my students seeking answers about what Vatican II meant. This was not possible since all the documents would not be published for a few years. Well-known commentators gave their opinions, a number of them contradicting each other. It would require faith and patience to weave through the challenges.

Aside from the work of the Council, there were controversial religious best-sellers that caught the attention of many students, among them Harvey Cox's *Secular City* and Anglican Bishop John Robinson's *Honest to God*. Cox's book upheld the merits of secularity. His exciting prose failed to observe the shortcomings of secularism, which is now quite evident to us. Robinson's folksy book undermined the supernatural nature of Christianity and fed into the "Death of God" movement, celebrated in *TIME* magazine's Easter cover that year.

Years later, I was in New York City to deliver the Good Friday meditations on Christ's "Seven Last Words" at St. Thomas the Apostle Church, a charming brownstone Gothic building formerly owned by the Episcopalians. When I announced the fourth word, "My God, my God, why have you forsaken me," I reminded the congregation about *TIME*'s 1966 Easter black cover framed in red, with the red-print title, "Is God Dead?" The editors said that the question tantalizes both believers who secretly feel God is dead and atheists who possibly suspect the answer is no.

I voiced my disagreement with *TIME*'s interpretation. I argued that the issue is the experience of God's presence, not existence. I proposed that in his fourth word, borrowed from Psalm 22, Jesus referred to his experience of the absence of his Father's presence. In his human nature, Christ felt a sense of filial loss just when he wanted to experience his Father's assuring presence. He is saying, "I want to feel your presence . . . but, what I said at Gethsemane, I say again: 'Thy will be done.'"

Just as he assumed our physical sufferings, he also experienced our times when God's presence feels far away. Blessed Teresa of Calcutta tells us she endured this aridity for many years. By his wounds, physical and mental, we are healed. On Easter Sunday, I celebrated the 11:00 a.m. Mass. Afterwards, a lady said, to me, "I liked your Good Friday talks, but my husband has a bone to pick with you." It turned out that he wrote the *TIME* cover story I was criticizing. Our meeting was brief and friendly and we both knew there wasn't enough time to do more than acknowledge a deeper dialogue would be needed. But it never happened.

In my course on the history of catechesis, I dealt with St. Augustine's little book on teaching religion, *Catechesi Tradendae* (On Catechesis). One of his comments stuck with me. He wrote that he often experienced enthusiasm about a topic while writing at his desk, only to feel empty when preaching the same idea. I also referred to the diary of the Lady Egeria, whose travels brought her to Jerusalem where she documented the process for training and welcoming converts to our Church, an ancient version of RCIA. I cited the great success of the Roman Catechism, commissioned by Pope St. Pius V, in 1566, as our response to Protestantism. It was not a question-answer catechism, but a narrative that reflected the decisions of the Council of Trent and set a model of Creed, Code, and Cult: The essential beliefs of the faith, the moral teachings of the Church, and the seven sacraments. It was an enduring sourcebook until its final edition in 1978.

I also dwelt on the origins of popularized catechisms as traced to Luther's success with that approach. For teaching religion to young people at various levels, St. Peter Canisius (1521–1597) in Germany and St. Robert Bellarmine (1542–1621) in Italy wrote question and answer catechisms in imitation of Luther's method. They based their content on the Roman Catechism. Both authors were incredibly successful. Canisius published his catechism in 1566. It had two hundred twenty-three questions and answers. In his own lifetime, it went through two hundred editions and was translated widely. In nineteenth century Germany, Canisius and catechism were synonymous. Bellarmine published a short catechism in 1597. For the next three centuries, his catechism was the most widely translated Catholic religion book after the Bible and Thomas a' Kempis' (1380–1471) *Imitation of Christ*. I did not know in 1966 that Saint John Paul II would commission a new Catechism of the Catholic Church first published in French 1992 and in English in 1994. I situated my courses for the graduate students in the light of Lumen Vitae's four sources for teaching religion.

Among the students I taught in those three years, two

of them became lifelong friends. Father Francis Kelly, (now a monsignor) and Father James Hawker. Before spending thirteen years as a distinguished leader of religious education at the National Catholic Educational Association (NCEA), Father Kelly was Director of Religious Education for the diocese of Worcester, MA. Father Hawker held a similar post in the archdiocese of Boston for twenty years. He later held the same post in the diocese of Charlotte for another ten years, while also serving as pastor of a growing suburban parish in Mint Hill. Father Hawker has since retired, but actively assists at Our Lady of Good Comfort parish in Waltham, MA, whose pastor is the dynamic Father James Di Perri. Both priests, when younger, lived and ministered at Sacred Heart Parish in Quincy, MA.

My life story is intimately bound up with my friendship with Francis Kelly. It began with his being my student at CUA. It continued when he served as a member of my board of advisers at NCEA. Then he succeeded me there for thirteen years. Our future contact was refreshed with summer vacations every year since and then a ten-year link at Blessed John Seminary where he was the rector and I was a professor.

I received many blessings from Msgr. Kelly's personal life of contemplative prayer. He was strongly devoted to the spiritual life, especially the spirituality of the Trappist Order, particularly Spencer Abbey in his diocese. He often spent a weekend retreat there when possible. Another practice he followed was making his annual retreat at a Trappist Abbey. In the years he has been in Europe, he has lined up retreats at such Abbeys in various countries. He remains faithful to daily meditation as well as the Mass and Liturgy of the Hours. There is a side to him that resonates with Irish austerity, but I hasten to add he is full of Irish laughter and knows how to have a good time. I will have more to write about him as time goes on. Our relationship flourished with God's graces and blessings.

After his ten-year leadership of Blessed John Seminary, Monsignor Kelly became Rector of the Casa Santa Maria in Rome. It is a residence for American priests obtaining advanced degrees in Rome. Recently, Monsignor Kelly has been appointed a Canon of St. Peter's Basilica in Vatican City. Canons conduct morning and evening prayer in choir as well as Sunday Mass and preaching, along with presence at papal ceremonies. We continue to stay in touch by phone and summer visits together. Monsignor Kelly and Father Hawker are like brothers to me.

You may have noticed that I often refer to friendships. I suppose this is not unusual. Augustine yearned for friendships, writing occasionally that he thanked God for sending friends into his life. I, too, am grateful for the many friendships I made over the years.

Another friend I made while at Catholic University was Father Leo Farley, who lived on my floor at Caldwell Hall. He was from Newark, NJ, and specialized in moral theology, which he had been teaching at the Newark archdiocesan seminary before teaching it at the university. He was as an original thinker, a man who lived the highest standards of the moral life. He was scholarly, though not given to quoting all kinds of writers. He had a great sense of humor and an uncanny connection to the everyday life of people. He had street smarts.

Gradually, we found ourselves meeting before supper to have a refreshment and talk about the day. One of the things I admired so much was his devotion to his mother and family. Every Friday afternoon, he drove to New Jersey to look in on his widowed mother. He checked on her needs and did what he could to help. He also helped with Sunday Masses at the parish in her town. As time went by, I got into the habit of waiting for him to return early Sunday evenings. Then we would go to a restaurant for dinner. This custom continued for the next six years. In the turmoil that began in my second year at the school, I valued his insights, though, unfortunately, I did not always apply them to my situation.

CHAPTER TWELVE

Storms at Sea and at the University

They who sailed the sea in ships . . . These saw
    the works of the Lord.
His command raised up a storm wind, which
    tossed its waves on high.
They mounted up to heaven; they sank to the
    depths.
They reeled and staggered like drunken men.
All their skill was swallowed up.

                  —Psalm 107: 23–27

A T the beginning of my second year at CUA in the autumn of 1966, I slowly became aware of unrest in the theology faculty. I had met Father Charles Curran a number of times. He was very pleasant and made me feel at home. Still, I had heard bits and pieces about his application for tenure and objections from some in the administration who were concerned about his favorable approach to artificial contraception. Matters came to a head in the spring. Curran had passed the requirements for tenure as an associate professor, but the Rector, Bishop McDonald, denied him tenure. I don't recall what reasons, if any, he offered. After much discussion, the majority of the faculty voted to strike in protest to the decision concerning Charles Curran.

The topic was about academic freedom, rather than the subject of birth control. But it was the elephant in the room. From April 19 through April 24, 1967, all classes were canceled. I gave a talk on behalf of Curran on the steps of Curley Hall where the Rector and tenured priest faculty members lived. I also marched in a picket line, carrying a placard in Curran's defense. The media was on campus every day, looking for news and interviews. On April 24, Cardinal O'Boyle, chancellor of the university, stood on the steps in front of the library, facing thousands of students and the media. He reversed the denial of tenure and restored Curran to the title of Associate Professor at the university.

That weekend there was a "victory Mass" held in the chapel of Trinity College across the street from campus. I was asked to deliver the homily. I recall saying that the Holy Spirit guided the decision to sponsor a strike in defense of Father Curran. I also remember a number of priests, somewhat angrily, telling me the Spirit had nothing to do with it. It was human courage that inspired the faculty and students to rally for justice in the case of Charles Curran. It was all politics. This was a small wake-up call to start questioning where I would stand in the future. In fact, the Holy Spirit had begun chipping away at me with a number of events shaping my future. However, I had a long way to go. This was painfully evident the following year.

Two events clouded the spring and summer of 1968.

On April 4, I was giving a Holy Week retreat to the seminarians at Holy Cross College, just up the street from the university. In the middle of the retreat, we received the news of the assassination of Dr. Martin Luther King. Violence had already begun on 7th and 14th Streets, the business and shopping districts in the area of Washington DC, densely populated with African Americans. I was advised to stop the retreat and get back to Caldwell Hall and found that the university was planning to suspend classes. Leo and I, however, went downtown for dinner and even went to a film. When we left the theater around 9:00 p.m., we saw the streets were empty and soldiers were patrolling the city in tanks and supervising the curfew. The capitol of the free world was at a temporary standstill. A policeman approached us and ordered us to get home as fast as possible, which we did.

For a full week, we were stranded at the university. We watched the events on TV during the day, and from the roof of Caldwell Hall we beheld Washington DC, on fire at night. A number of priests ventured out to help people in need. This chaotic conclusion formed a tragic contrast to Rev. King's glorious "I Have Dream" speech on the National Mall on August 28, 1963. His words were consoling, his murder a disgrace. I remember driving with two of the student priests on Easter Sunday through 7th and 14th Streets. Hundreds of stores were burnt out, windows were smashed, and a blanket of despair dulled the Alleluia's of the feast. It took years to restore some of these streets.

The Pope and the Pill

> The transmission of human life is a most serious role in which married people collaborate freely and responsibly with God the Creator. It has always been a source of great joy to them, even though it sometimes entails many difficulties and hardships.
>
> Pope Paul VI, *Humanae Vitae*, the opening lines.

The second storm of those rocky days arrived only a few months later, July 19, 1968, when Pope Paul VI issued his encyclical, *Humanae Vitae*. The pope repeated the Church's teaching on married life and condemned the use of artificial contraception. He defended the competence of the magisterium to resolve the issue, cited the principles to be followed, and supplied pastoral guidance. He emphasized that his teaching was entirely in accord with the decrees of Vatican II. It created an uproar at the university and some faculty members began signing a petition of protest.

I was among them, even though I had not yet read the document, nor taken the time to dwell on Pope Paul's teaching about the role of the magisterium. Swept up by emotion, I went along with the crowd, failing to reflect on the formation of my conscience in so serious a matter. As I look back on it, I wonder how I arrived at this point. In my seminary days, I was a disciple of the Jesuit motto, "Live the mind of the Church. Support the pope!"

The winds of the sixties affected so many of us, myself included.

What happened to that ideal? I am not proud of what happened and regret, to this day, my complicity in the affair. In the following year, there were discussions about dismissing faculty members who signed the protest, but it never came to fruition. I began using one of Sister Bart's one liners, "O Lord, be merciful to me a sinner."

I had become a collector of scripture texts as prayers, some of which I taped near the mirror in my bathroom. I knew that loss of humility is always a trap for the soul. I needed God's reminder who puts on my lips these words in Psalm 131, used also in the Liturgy of Hours for Tuesday evening prayer. I pray these words, not because they are true of me, but because they ought to be:

> O Lord, my heart is not proud
>> nor haughty my eyes.
> I have not gone after things too great
>> nor marvels beyond me.
> Truly, I have set my soul
>> in silence and peace.
> As a child has rest in his mother's arms.
>> even so my soul.
>> (Psalm 131:1–2
>> Liturgy of the Hours, Volume Three,
>> Saturday Office of Readings, Week One)

At that time, I was beginning my last year as a visiting professor and started thinking of studying for a doctorate in religious education. My patron, Father Sloyan, had insisted on my considering this plan. He had left Catholic University and had been hired with tenure by Temple University in Philadelphia. Franciscan Father Berard Marthaler was the new head of my department at CUA. I asked him if I would be welcome as a doctoral student. He said he would bring my request to the faculty. After a long period I received their support for seeking a doctorate. I went through the process for application and, in time, received the good news that the university would award me a full scholarship of room, board, and tuition. Abbot Killeen approved my quest for the doctorate as well.

The Process of Conversion

"Though often foolishly I strayed, yet in your love you sought me.

You taught me to be unafraid, and home again you brought me."

—"The King of Love," Hymn

A violent squall came up and waves were breaking over the boat. Jesus was in the stern, asleep on a cushion. They woke him and said, "Teacher! Do you not care that we are perishing?" He woke up, rebuked the wind, and said to the sea, "Quiet! Be still!" The wind ceased and there was great calm.

—Mark 4:37–39

He hushed the storm to a gentle breeze, and the
billows of the sea were stilled."

—Psalm 107:29

Repent! For the kingdom of heaven is at hand.

—Matthew, 3:2

The tumult during my three years of teaching at Catholic
University had tested my faith, my identity as a priest, my
commitment to the Church and her teachings. It was not
the fault of the school, which I loved. Shakespeare had it
right: "The fault lies not in the stars, dear Brutus, but in
ourselves." Or, perhaps, you like the cartoon Pogo's way
of delivering this sentiment: "We have met the enemy
and it is us." I have met the enemy and it was me. Over
the course of thirty-six months, I had feasted on a diet of
protest, questioning, doubt, infidelity, nuns leaving their
habits home, priests dating nuns, marrying them, and
giving up their vows. God gave me the rock of Father Leo
Farley whose wisdom curtailed my erratic enthusiasms,
though I think Leo would reject this claim.

I participated in the chaos. I joined a group favor-
ing married priests. But once I saw the immediate flood
of infidelity to the Church, I regretted my support and
abandoned it, because it was a sign both of my own
unfaithful leanings and of my misguided participation in
advancing this cause. In that brief pause between three
years of teaching and three years of post-graduate study,
I welcomed what I now see was a process of conversion.

Our Lord and his Mother had other plans for me, and, thanks be to God's mercy, they prevailed.

The tipping point occurred when the "messiah" of dissent, Hans Kung, arrived at the campus to deliver a pep talk about a new kind of church. Cardinal O'Boyle opposed his appearance, but to no avail. So great was the anticipated crowd, that Kung was given the gymnasium for his platform. I had read his book, *The Council Reform and Reunion*, and liked it, but it was tame compared to the program of dissent Kung subsequently began to proclaim. Prior to his talk, I sat across from him at dinner in Curley Hall. He was a charming guest. He saved his rhetoric for the speech.

I did not attend his talk, but stood in the midst of the crowd who could not get into the gym. As he came into view, he was greeted with cheers and a flurry of camera flashes. He was regarded as a theological rock star. My friend Father Francis Kelly was with me, and heard me say in a pretended German accent, "Today, Washington, tomorrow, the world!" Monsignor Kelly still reminds me of my comment. That night was my version of the poet John Donne's line, "Do not ask for whom the bell tolls. It tolls for thee." My illusions were fading as the bell tolled. Christ and his Mother were successfully pulling me away from a fruitless future and I am eternally grateful.

Centuries ago Jesus predicted such events. "If anyone says to you then, 'Look, here is the Messiah!' or, 'There he is!' do not believe it. False prophets and false messiahs will arise, and they will perform signs and wonders so great as to deceive, if that were possible, even the elect." (Matthew 24:23–24). It was a time of tumult and confusion. Kung's dissent was rampant, even, perhaps especially, on the campus of America's flagship Catholic university.

By contrast, Jesuit Avery Dulles, one day to become a cardinal, gradually went public on the issue of dissent. His biographer, Patrick Carey, has this to report about Dulles:

> By the late 1980's Dulles believed that the culture of dissent and, what Hans Urs von Balthasar had called a 'venomous and irrational Anti-Roman feeling' had emerged to a considerable extent in American Catholicism and in the Catholic theological community. Although Dulles continued to acknowledge a role for differing theological opinions . . . he worked against what he believed to be an unhealthy and pervasive mentality of dissent . . . Within this context, he repeatedly advised giving the benefit of the doubt to magisterial statements, exercising thereby a hermeneutic of trust rather than of suspicion.
>
> (*Avery Cardinal Dulles, a Model Theologian*, by Patrick W. Carey, Paulist Press, New York, 2010, page 422.)

Thankfully, the tide has turned, to some extent, with the eloquent leadership of Popes John Paul II and Benedict XVI. Pope John Paul's sponsorship of the Catechism of the Catholic Church was a pastoral landmark for guidance to all teachers and preachers of the faith. His world-wide rallies for the faith, especially World Youth Days, have aroused the rebirth of faith. However the influence of Catholic dissenters has found an ally in the rise of aggressive secularism appearing now in the halls of political power and attempting to erase the faith from the public square. Pope Benedict has promoted the pastoral response of a "New Evangelization" especially for industrialized nations in Europe and the United States, which have become a kind of mission territory. Pope John Paul became the first new missionary to the entire world. Pope Benedict, for his part, led all Catholics to become aware of their missionary vocation. His "Year of Faith" is designed for mission awareness.

Pope Benedict treated Kung graciously at the beginning of his papacy by inviting him for a personal visit. Kung repaid the pope's hospitality by pursuing his campaign for dissent. I gather that Benedict prays for Kung's conversion and I gladly join that prayer.

While dissent was swirling, I determined to distance myself from it and focus on the doctoral program. I discovered that one of the great advantages of doctoral studies is that they produce a tranquilizing effect. The three years of study and writing of a dissertation were, in many ways, like a long retreat, which served as a spur to reflection after the distracting and distressing events I experienced. I bypassed the master's thesis, but attended all the classes and did the papers and exams. After that, I completed the classroom work for the doctorate and faced comprehensive exams. My symbolic storms at sea were about to subside for a time.

Our doctoral exams took place in a university house where we each had a room and a supervisor was on duty. I passed, but only after a conversation with one of the faculty members who quizzed me on one of the issues. I had been blessed with the professors who taught me. They had had a calming effect on me, mainly by their positive attitudes and fair-minded presentations of the teachings of the Church and their catechetical applications. Doctrine, liturgy, scripture, history, psychology had been taught with substance.

I had a difficult time choosing a topic for my dissertation. My first two proposals were rejected. At first, I thought that a thesis comparing an American poet's religious outlook with the Catholic one and benefit catechesis might pass. The English department refused, claiming I did not have enough depth in that area. The same argument shot down my second proposal, namely, to contrast the thought of a German philosopher Hubert Halbfas with Catholic vision and catechesis. In hindsight, they were right to reject my proposals.

In one of my pre-supper discussions with Leo Farley I conveyed my disappointment. Out of nowhere, he said, "Why don't you propose a study about Rabbi Abraham Heschel. You like him. You have heard his talks at the Washington Synagogue. He is both a philosopher and a noted teacher of religion. You have read a number of his books and always seem excited about him." I agreed with him, wrote the proposal, and it was accepted. I gave it a heavy-handed title: "The Transcendental Themes of Rabbi Abraham Heschel and Their Value for Catholic Catechesis."

I needed to have a director whose specialty was scripture, and also a reader who understood the religious teachings and customs of the Jewish community, especially those who follow the Hasidic form of Judaism. Father Marthaler appointed a Carmelite scripture scholar to chair the dissertation committee. I sought out Aileen Grognet to be a reader. In fact she was mainly my director. She was a convert from Judaism to Catholicism through the help of Archbishop Hallinan of Atlanta. Her knowledge of the teachings and customs of the Jewish faith helped me with my understanding of Rabbi Heschel. The Department of Religious Education at Catholic University approved her as a consultant. The Department also appointed her to the board of examiners that approved my reception of a doctorate in Religious Education. I remain very grateful for her excellent advice.

Her Jewish background helped me greatly in understanding the mindset of Rabbi Heschel. She agreed to be a reader and was very helpful to me with the details of Heschel's career and ministry. I thank God also for her defense of my approach to Heschel after my grilling by the dissertation committee. At a celebratory lunch with Aileen, we raised a glass of champagne and she said, "L'Chaim, To Life."

Heschel was born a Polish-born Jew, but after the rise of the Nazis he moved to the United States and became a citizen in 1945. After several visiting professorships, he joined the faculty of Union Theological Seminary in New York City. His books, *Man is not Alone* and *God in Search of Man*, introduced him to a wide reading audience. In his other books and dozens of articles, he combines a reverent fidelity to his Hasidic background with a respect for modern scholarship and discovery. He binds authentic piety and intellectual demands. He has a great deal to give to our religious educators, caught as we are between the teachings of tradition and the need to find contemporary expressions of faith.

He applied his wisdom to the everyday challenges of a religious educator. He also placed such ministry in the tension between the immanent, the earthly side of what we do, and the transcendent, God's active presence in our daily lives. In an endless number of creative ways, he resolves the tension by pushing us to keep both dimensions of the divine and human in creative presence with each other.

The path that Heschel opened to me was the contrast between immanence and the transcendent. This was the key that I used to write the dissertation, but also to rewrite my own way of approaching the dilemmas of the Sixties and incredibly still bothering all us in the first decades of the twenty first century.

Heschel was perfectly aware of the world of immanence. He saw its pleasant side in the world of secular learning at the university of Berlin where he studied modern philosophy. He experienced its bitter side when he was forced to leave his native Poland because of the Nazis. As an American citizen he embraced "immanent" causes of peace, race, and poverty. But he also was committed to the transcendent. For him, deep, personal prayer was no embarrassment. He could discourse on the presence of God (transcendence) with feeling, faith, and conviction. He was a modern Rabbi, who made tradition seem so real that you could touch it.

Above: The Dougherty's. *Back Row:* Larry, Anne, Edward. *Front Row:* Therese, Catherine, Patricia and her baby Kimberly. *Below:* Sanctuary of St. Patrick's Catholic Church.

Above: My Mom Mary Courtney and her sister Elizabeth Corcoran. *Below*: Abbot Pennings, Founder of St. Norbet Abbey, in his 90s, blessing a novice. *Opposite*: Me as a seminarian at St. Norbert College.

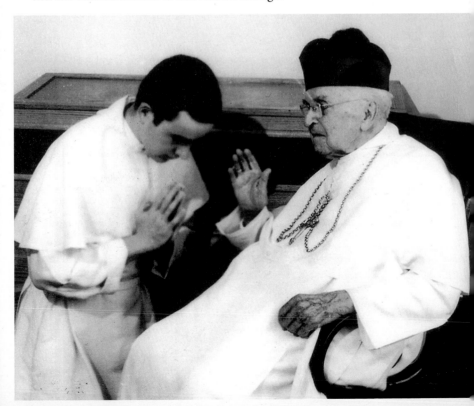

Above: St. Norbert College (BAs in Philo. And English). *Left:* Brochure of St. Norbert College.

Above: My ordination class. We were ordained in St. Edmund's Church South Philadelphia on June 20, 1953 by Archbishop John O'Hara. *From L to R:* Fathers Robert Kelly, Henry Jafolla, Pastor, Abbot Sylvester Killeen, O. Praem., Neil McLauhglin (formation director), John Cox, me, Vincent Conway. *Right:* Pastor Blaise J. Peters, O Praem. St. Joseph Chruch

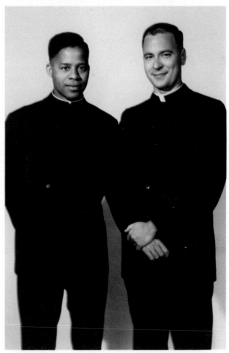

Above: Interior of St. Joseph Church *Left:* At Lumen Vitae 1963. Brussels, Belgium. My best student and friend, Fr. Fabian Kapufi from Tanzania. *Opposite:* Me giving a lecture to an assembly of 1000 School Sisters of Notre Dame in 1965.

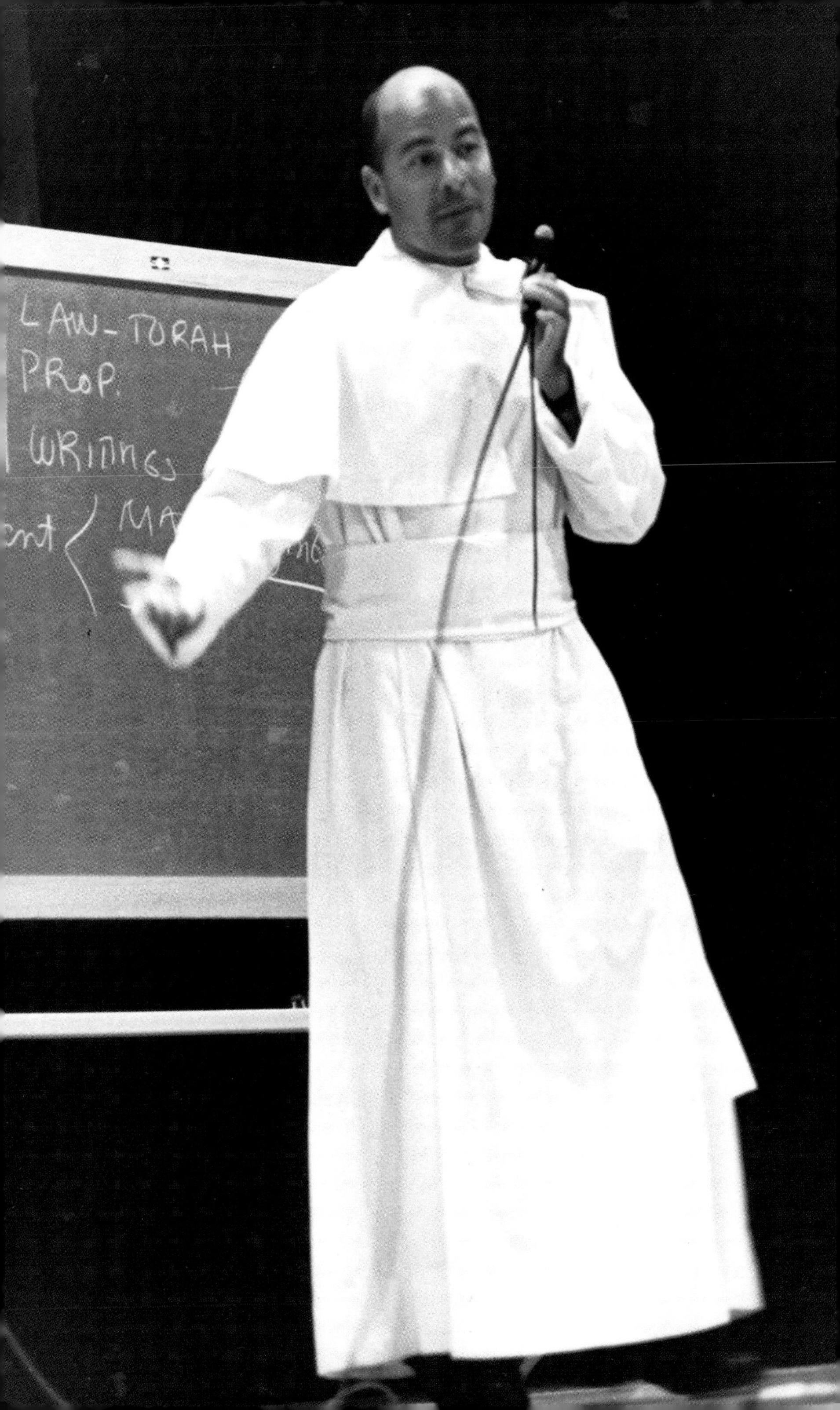
LAW-TORAH
PROP.
WRITINGS

Above: Msgr. Francis Kelly, Msgr. Michael Carroll, Fr. James Hawker, Msgr. Michael Foley, John Foley, Tim Murphy, and Me. Fr. John Forliti was on a trip to Africa at this time.

Below: New St. Norbert Abbey building in 1959.

Above: Norbertine Center for spirituality.
Below: Mother Therese of Spirit of Love—my prayer partner for 25 years, Carmelite Sister in Sioux City, IA.

Above: Fr. John Bradley addresses my college board with Mrs. Gena McKee. *Left:* Al and Shannon.

Right: Archbishop Sanchez (Me as pres. Of Univ. of Albany. *Below:* Presidential Reflections.

Above: Golden Jubilee of priesthood in front of St. Patrick's Church in Philadelphia. With family-all cousins. To my right is Anne Dougherty and on my left is Therese Dougherty and her son Ciaran Dougherty. In the next row is Edward Dougherty (Anne's husband) and their son Lared. Next is Larry Dougherty, Therese's husband. Next comes Mary McEvoy and her husband Finbar who live in Berwyn, Philadelphia suburb. All others are from Coronado, CA. *Below:* St. Norbert College magazine. *Opposite:* Newspaper article.

"That vast assembly had made a lot of sacrifice, all of them

Newman would say, use your reason as far as you can go with it, then use your faith as far as you can go with it, and then integrate the two."

This was McBride's first encounter with Pope Benedict XVI, but the Norbertine served as a representative of the Catholic bishops at the visit of John Paul II to the United States in 1987. ✢

The Rev. Alfred McBride stands on the grounds outside the St. Norbert Abbey Church in De Pere. The National Conference for Catechetical Leadership will grant its annual award to McBride on May 25. PHOTOS BY EVAN SIEGLE/PRESS-GAZETTE

Rev. McBride will be honored with award

Event to recognize St. Norbert Abbey priest is May 25

By Judy Turba
Special to the Press-Gazette

The National Conference for Catechetical Leadership will grant its annual award to the Rev. Alfred McBride, a priest at St. Norbert Abbey, on May 25 at its meeting in Atlanta.

Leland Nagel, executive director of the group, said in an announcement, "The Award exemplifies the commitment of Father McBride to present the beliefs of the Catholic faith in a language that can be understood by the adults whose responsibility is to pass on the faith they received at Baptism. His writings, especially the popular Teen Catechism, also ministers to adolescents who desperately seek the truth."

Officials at St. Norbert Abbey are excited one of their own is being recognized.

"We have always valued Father McBride's contributions to religious education and are delighted he is receiving this much deserved award," said the Rev. James Herring, O. Praem. "Through his faith and writings he has touched the souls of thousands of people throughout this country and beyond. His work and recognition bring honor to all of us."

A member of St. Norbert Abbey, McBride lives at St. Joseph Priory on the campus of St. Norbert College. For most of his 58 years as a priest and teacher, he has been involved in religious education. He obtained a doctorate in this field from the Catholic University of America. Soon thereafter, he found-

The Rev. Alfred McBride celebrates Mass and preaches on Relevant Radio each Wednesday.

ed the department of religious education at the National Catholic Education Association.

Throughout the years his ministry included writing 40 books and more than 200 articles on topics ranging from Church history, the lives of the saints, the interpretation of the Gospels, explanations of the Catechism of the Catholic Church, how to pray like Jesus and the saints, a short history of the Mass and six volumes of homilies. His recent publications include, "A Priest Forever," called a "gem of a book," by Jesuit Father James Martin, and "Staying Faithful Today," a plea for fidelity to our promises in our throwaway culture.

McBride has hosted a number of 13-part series on the Catholic television network, EWTN, on subjects dealing with the mysteries of the Book of Revelation, the life and teachings of Pope John XXIII and the teachings of the Church regarding Mary, the mother of Jesus.

As a professor for nine years at Blessed John XXIII Seminary, he taught preaching to late vocation seminarians. McBride subsequently wrote a book, "How to Make Homilies Better, Briefer, Bolder." In the introduction to the book,

Archbishop Timothy Dolan writes, "My own study of Church history has led me to conclude that every period of genuine renewal in the Church has been characterized by a revival of sound preaching." McBride celebrates Mass and preaches on Relevant Radio each Wednesday.

One of McBride's fondest memories is related to his role in the second pastoral visit of Blessed John Paul II to the United States. The American bishops appointed him spokesman during the visit. He said that while he was available for interviews, he also attended one event each day. He said he would never forget the meeting with the leaders of the media at Sheraton Universal Studios, who watched the most touching encounter of the visit while waiting for the pope to speak to them.

McBride said, "Those who recall the visit will always remember the pope's reaction to the song by Tony Melendez, who was born without arms. He played his guitar with his toes and sang an original song for the Holy Father. John Paul was so moved that he jumped off the podium and wrapped his arms around the man without arms. Tony's face was pure joy. I noted the prolonged silence of the 300 business leaders. It was a human touch that no movie or TV show could surpass."

The Catechetical Leadership award states, "Father McBride has zealously promoted catechesis for decades through his teaching, writing and speaking. He has been a sterling example of dedication and fruitfulness in this great work of catechesis."

McBride is deeply moved and grateful for the award from our nation's leaders in religious education.

Judy Turba is the public relations coordinator at St. Norbert Abbey in De Pere.

Above: Shaking hands with John Paul II during his second pastoral visit to the United States in 1987. *Below:* With Mother Theresa and Fr. John Meyers (President of the NCEA: National Catholic Education Association). We are inviting her to our next convention in New York City. She accepted. 1985.

Above: With President Ronald Reagan, giving a NCEA talk. *Below:* With Mother Angelica at the conclusion of my 13-part series on the life and teachings of Pope John XXIII. 1989.

Above: George H.W. Bush. Rented our campus for a fundraiser. *Right:* Bob Moccia and his wife Ria.

CHAPTER THIRTEEN

An Unexpected Call
The NCEA

Teachers must remember that it depends chiefly on them whether or not the Catholic school achieves its purpose. Possessed by charity both towards each other and towards their students. Inspired by an apostolic spirit, they should bear testimony, by their lives and their teaching, to the one Teacher who is Christ.

—Vatican II Declaration on Christian Education,
Paragraph 8

The definitive aim of catechesis is to put people not only in touch but also in communion and in intimacy with Jesus Christ. The primary and essential object of catechesis is, to use an expression dear to St. Paul, "the mystery of Christ." It is to seek and understand the meaning of Christ's actions and words, and of the signs worked by him.

—*On Catechesis in Our Time,*
John Paul II, 5

During my last year at Catholic University, Sister Sarah Fassenmeier, Dean of the School of Education, invited me to serve on a panel that was developing a booklet, "The Competencies and Qualities of a Religion Teacher." It was a collaborative project with the National Catholic Educational Association (NCEA), a professional society for the various leaders of Catholic schools and colleges and parish religious education offices. One of the members of the panel was Monsignor John (Jack) Meyers, Director of NCEA's office for Diocesan Superintendents of Catholic Schools. During the proceedings, we came to know each other and have remained lifelong friends. The document we completed was published as a booklet by the NCEA and was a bestseller for a number of years.

After our last meeting, Jack invited me to dinner with him. During the meal, he asked me what I was going to do with my doctorate. I said that I was planning to return to our Abbey and perhaps teach at St. Norbert College. He replied, "Why don't you come to NCEA and be the founder of our planned office of religious education?" He went on to speak about the changes occurring Catholic schools at both the secondary and elementary levels. With thousands of sisters and male religious leaving the convents, monasteries, and schools, there was an influx of lay teachers and principals for whom a service in religious education and the Catholicity of the schools would be a demand.

He described how the other major changes in the areas of scripture, doctrine, and liturgy since the publication of the documents of Vatican II had led to the development of new texts and methods for teaching religion. The field needed national guidance, support, and direction in these areas. As I listened to him I thought of what I had experienced those last six years teaching and studying. I had not reflected on how what I had seen and heard would affect Catholic education, but it became clear.

I had been aware of the NCEA since one of our Norbertine priests, Father Albert Koob, was its president. I knew him from the days when he was a teacher at Southeast Catholic and I was a student there, though I never had him in class. I asked Jack if the staff would object to another Norbertine coming aboard. Jack told me that would not be a problem. I was thrilled with the invitation and wondered what Abbot Killeen would think. I need not have worried. Abbot Killeen was even more enthusiastic than I was. So, in September 1971, I joined the NCEA for the most interesting years of my life. I had a lot to learn and the staff was patiently willing to guide me through the complexities of a national organization, but it was well worth it and I enjoyed the training, despite my stumbles.

I rented a first-floor apartment on Corcoran Street from a Benedictine priest who was hoping to become a diocesan priest. It was a five-minute walk to the NCEA's offices in Dupont Circle.

Four weeks after my arrival at NCEA, a tragedy occurred. Father Koob was planning a trip to Majorca where an international Catholic education conference was about to convene. On the warm, autumn evening before his departure, he celebrated a home Mass at the house of his secretary, Nancy Brewer and her mother, in the Spring Valley neighborhood. After supper he suggested that he and Nancy take a walk to see a nearby series of new upscale shops that would soon open. As they walked along they came to a shop in the front of which was a sidewalk with a metal grate over a deep empty space, something often seen in cities. Unaware that the grate was not correctly attached to the surrounding cement, Father Koob stepped on the screen. It collapsed and he went with it, dropping thirty feet.

He was seriously injured. When we visited him the next day, he was unconscious and much of his body was swollen from the injuries. After six weeks of recovery in the hospital he was able to return to his office. He used a cane but needed therapy for his shoulders and other parts of his body. However the shock to his system was so great that he had to resign. It was a sad time for him and the staff. He returned to the Norbertine Abbey in Paoli, PA where he spent the rest of his life. The NCEA board appointed Jack Meyers as the new president, an office he served with distinction for the next fifteen years.

One of my duties at NCEA was organizing and conducting seminars for members in the field. My first seminar was for a group of parish directors of religious education on the west coast. In those days, this was a new contribution to parishes by laity with degrees in religious education and dedicated to the mission of faith for youth and adults. A number of them were former sisters who were more accustomed to parish needs and very helpful. Time and patience were needed to develop relationships with pastors and other parish leaders. Our seminar was held in one of the meeting rooms in the crypt of the San Francisco Cathedral. The facilities were new, spacious, and welcoming. Jack Meyers came with me to guide me through the process. There were about one hundred participants from northern California, Oregon, and Washington. After all the welcomes and Jack's generous introduction, I passed out an outline of how the three days would be spent.

I had barely finished when a number of hands went up. Several of the seminar attendees told me that the content and sequence was unsatisfactory. I was tempted to argue with them, but as a rookie with a dose of prudence, I felt I should listen. I encouraged them to explain in more detail what they wanted, most of which made sense. Gradually, I came around and said that they should write up a new schedule and development. Jack was sitting in the back, seemingly having a good time smiling from ear to ear through the whole experience.

I gave them time to create a new approach and called for hands to volunteer for the work. I then sat with those engaged in the task and when I saw the new recommendations I was pleased, because the plan was more relevant to their immediate needs and was a teaching tool for me. Still, it was a drain. But I chalked it up to a learning experience. They enlightened me about issues such as decent salaries, support from pastors, setting goals for proper degrees for all members, cooperation with Catholic school administrators and faculty, in addition to other things. Jack was pleased with the outcome. Over the years, I started the National Organization of Parish Coordinators and Directors (NPCD), with their own board and newsletters. It had its growing pains, but it still flourishes. I attended, as a guest, their 35th Anniversary banquet in New Orleans amid lots of hugs and welcomes. May God love them.

I had spent most of my life around Catholic schools both as a student and a teacher, but I was not aware of the tensions between parish school staffs and the volunteers who taught religion to students from the public schools. At the time, the popular name for this mission was "Confraternity of Christian Doctrine" or CCD. Even in my first four years as an assistant in a parish, I did not notice any difficulties, probably because I relied on the generosity and talent of Catholic public high school teachers who were parishioners and who taught our high school religion classes with great success. In addition, our sisters taught classes for the elementary age students on Saturdays.

Creative Contributions by Diocesan Directors

Jack Meyers had been thinking of responding to the needs of the diocesan directors for religious education in both schools and parishes and he commissioned me to start a national association for these directors. We had meetings with key directors who already were active in advancing this vision. The discussions were lively and resulted in the founding of the National Association of Diocesan Directors of Religious Education (NCDRE). I set up an advisory board that included these priests: Fr. Francis Kelly of Worcester, MA, Fr. James Hawker of Boston, MA, (my former students from Catholic University), Fr. Michael Carroll from Philadelphia, PA, Fr. Tom Sullivan from Chicago, IL, Fr. John Forliti of St. Paul, MN, Fr. Ron Amandolare from Paterson, NJ. More were added as time passed.

One of the NCDRE's unique projects was an annual meeting in which participants worked on the ideas and content of a projected booklet to be published by NCEA. Somewhat like a think-tank, they tried to figure out the immediate needs for religious education. Several of their concepts grew out of research that was capturing the imagination of religion teachers who liked what they saw, but could use guidance within the teachings of the Church. Three of those issues were rooted in studies from developmental psychology. The preferred imagery was expressed as stages of faith by James Fowler and stages of moral development by Lawrence Kohlberg. Even more provocative and popular was Sidney Simon's Values Clarification, which used "games" to disclose the moral preferences of students.

Our annual winter meetings of diocesan directors, usually held in warm climates, addressed these issues and provided the raw material for a booklet to be published by NCEA. I was assigned to be the writer. In those early years, our participants acknowledged the usefulness of stage theories for teaching morality and faith, and Simon's games as a lever for discovering one's values. But they also argued that the context for all of this should be the biblical and Church tradition of God's revelation of faith and moral standards, the role of grace, the training in virtues, and the presence of human freedom.

Our diocesan directors insisted that teachers should be flexible in dealing with stage theories, being careful to avoid forcing students into the models while ignoring the unique backgrounds of each individual. They also situated matters of faith and morals within the role of the covenant and commandments of Old Testament, as well as the Sermon on the Mount, other commands by Jesus, who fulfills the covenant, and commands of the Hebrew scripture. It would have helped immensely if the *Catechism of the Catholic Church*, published in 1992 under John Paul II's leadership, had been available to us in the 1970s.

Our study groups also raised called for virtue education based on objective truths of scripture, reason, and tradition to offset the subjective shortcomings of the "values" approach. This was an exciting time for the participants because of its relevance to key moments in our encounter with challenges to our faith and morals and the essential need to devote our energies to virtue education.

From REOI to ACRE
Raising Students' Commitment to Beliefs,
Attitudes and Practices

Another project in which I was involved was proposed by our staff educational research member, George Elford. He proposed the development of a test for eighth-grade students in Catholic schools, to evaluate their beliefs, attitudes, and practices. Elford would oversee the composition of the test in consultation with me and the board of diocesan directors. It was agreed that a national meeting would be convened to introduce the plan, to hear the objections, and to seek widespread approval. Initially, the objections and resistance to the concept were strong, but gradually trimmed back to a sufficient acceptance. From the first year of usage, till many years later, the value of this approach was a positive service to the teachers as well as the students in supporting their commitment to their faith, religious attitudes, and practices.

Several years after this project began, a similar test was offered for an earlier grade. Eventually the project became known as ACRE: Assessment of Catechesis/ Religious Education. It was designed to help school, parish and diocesan leaders evaluate the faith knowledge and attitudes of students in Catholic schools and parish-based religious programs. ACRE measures religious beliefs as it relates to God, the Church, Liturgy and Sacraments, Revelation, Life in Christ, Church History, Prayer/Religious Practices and Catholic Faith Literacy. In alternating years, children in grades five through eight are given the assessment test. This all developed after my final year at NCEA in 1979. I am happy to report that this service has been offered by the NCEA to Catholic schools and parish religious education programs for many years.

Our NCEA Mission: To Teach as Jesus Did

In 1972, the United States Conference of Catholic Bishops issued a pastoral message on Christian education, "To Teach as Jesus Did." The bishops directed their attention to the importance of education in the faith:

> Education is one of the most important ways by which the Church fulfills its commitment to the dignity of the person and the building of community. The educational efforts of the Church must therefore be directed to forming persons-in-community; for the education of the individual Christian is important not only to his solitary destiny but also to the destinies of the many communities in which he lives.
>
> While these three essential elements of Message, Community and Service can be separated for the sake of analysis, they are joined in the one educational ministry.

> *(To Teach as Jesus Did*, The United States Conference of Catholic Bishops, Daughters of St. Paul Publication, Boston, MA, 1972)

They built their pastoral letter around the three topics of Message, Community, and Service. The Message was the proclamation of the history of salvation foreseen in the covenant of God with his people Israel, taught by the prophets, and witnessed by the faithful. This revelation of salvation is fulfilled by the birth, teachings, witness, death, resurrection, and ascension of Jesus Christ, continued by the apostles, popes, bishops and all of God's holy people throughout their journey of faith throughout history. It is always accompanied by the formation of a community of faith, hope and love as well as service to the world:

> The experience of Christian community leads naturally to service. Christ gives His people different gifts not only for themselves but for others. Each must serve the other for the good of all. The Church is a servant community in which those who hunger are to be filled; the ignorant are to be taught; the homeless to receive shelter; the sick cared for; the distressed consoled; the oppressed set free—all so that men may more fully realize their human potential and more readily enjoy life with God now and eternally.

> But the Christian community should not be concerned only for itself. Christ did not intend it to live walled off from the world any more than He intended each person to work out his destiny in isolation from others. Fidelity to the

> will of Christ joins His community with the total
> human community.

Our staff was excited by this document, both for its potential for religious education as well as for the challenge to take it to the nation. After a number of discussions, we decided to create a traveling workshop that, eventually, would bring its message to twenty-five dioceses and archdioceses over a period of two years. We assembled a team that treated the topics of catechesis, faith-community building, the role of research, the challenge to administration, finances, the service of the Church's social teachings, and the faith formation of teachers.

Those two years were an exhilarating experience, both tiring and inspiring, as we viewed the Church in America through many lenses and realized the remarkable graces received by our listeners. We also grew closer as a team, and became more realistic back home, more prepared to serve our teachers, administrators, and students.

It was also a way to bridge the gap between ourselves and the mission of the bishops. They had the wisdom and grace to produce this profound teaching about message, community, and service and we had the tools to spread their pastoral efforts. Our modern journeys to bring the Gospel to American Catholic educators gave me the feeling that we were heirs of St. Paul's endless trips over Roman roads.

Interlude: My Oxford Winter

Midway through my nine years at NCEA, I obtained a brief winter sabbatical which I spent as a visiting student at Oxford University. My close friend, Father John Bradley, often spoke to me about his years at Oxford, obtaining the treasured degree in "Greats," a grueling course in Latin and Greek literature. He described various tutorials that assumed he was already familiar with the content of and discussions about the Greek and Latin classics, but he prevailed.

He also remembered with gratitude his rooms at Campion Hall, the Jesuit residence at the university. With his intercession, I was able to obtain a place to stay at Campion Hall during my studies at the university. Jesuit Father Winterborn was the house master and welcomed me warmly. One of the pleasures of the Hall was Guest Night, usually on Wednesdays. The festive evening began with sherry in the community room, then dinner, followed by port and dessert at small tables in the library next door. During the term many of us were invited to dessert with one of the guests. Our most famous guest was the former Prime Minister of England, Harold Macmillan. After supper he held court with us for over two hours, recalling the challenges he faced while in office, as well as his relationships with Churchill and President Kennedy.

Campion Hall is one block from the stunning Christ Church Cathedral. To my joy, I discovered that, every afternoon, the Cathedral held evensong. Almost every afternoon, I praised God with the outstanding men and boys choir as they sang the psalms of David and the stirring hymns of the Anglican Church in a Gothic setting. I loved walking through the campus, every inch an authentic medieval display of colleges and chapels, along with the famed Bodleian Library, the picturesque Sheldonian Theater and other auxiliary buildings that breathed the traditions of a centuries old university.

When I was making plans to go to Oxford, Barbara Murphy, an Irish-born secretary at NCEA, gave me the address of Sean O'Tuama, a close friend of hers who was a guest professor of Irish Language at the Welch College. He was a celebrated Irish poet and author of Irish language textbooks. Once I was settled in, I phoned him, gave him regards from Barbara and introduced myself. I suggested we get together over tea. He sounded cold and indifferent when he repeated, "Tea?" I was, for once, a quick learner: "Well, I would be honored to meet you and host you for scotch." That did it. We began a relationship that lasted throughout my days at Oxford. I figured he was an Irish anti-clerical, but we had ways to relate, especially when the topic of racquetball, my game, and squash, his game, came up. He taught me squash during a number of sweaty, challenging games for the rest of the term. We parted as friends and pledged to meet again. That's a story I will tell you later.

I gained many benefits from my time at Oxford. I learned that all the dons (professors), were asked to present a course of lectures in their specialty once a year that were open to the public free of charge. Father Winterborn lent me what looked like a phone book that outlined the vast number of offerings. I scanned the remarkable range of lectures and soon settled on "The Comedies of Shakespeare." The auditorium was packed and the professor, who had a career in acting, launched into his topics with enthusiasm as well as with all his dramatic skills. When he saw that large clock signaled the final two minutes, it always roused him to a powerful conclusion that stirred us all. I also took advantage of a course on the history of the first folios of Macbeth (heavy going) and a series delivered by a scrappy theologian of a Fundamentalist sect (heavier going). These courses were good, but I finally settled on a superb series given by Professor John Macquarrie, the Lady Margaret Professor of Divinity at Oxford, whose course was the highlight of my days at Oxford.

Unlike the other courses that had only one lecture a week, Macquarrie lectured superbly to an eager gathering of students three times a week. His topic sounded daunting, "Christology from Schleiermacher to the Present." In fact, he devoted the first couple of weeks to the Christology of the first four Councils of the Church. I wish his lectures had been taped, because of his evident faith and the clarity, depth, and truth of what he had to say. I still recall his last sentence of the lectures on the Councils. With his engaging Scots accent, he looked us in our eyes and said, "You see, these Councils are the basic building blocks of all Christology." A line from the

Divine Praises came back to me at that moment, "Blessed be Jesus Christ true God and true man." Macquarrie's insights into the Councils later accompanied me when I made a pilgrimage to the sites of the first four Councils.

Macquarrie held the title of "Lady Margaret Professor of Divinity" at Oxford. The title goes back to the years just before King Henry VIII started the Reformation in England. Bishop John Fisher was the head of Cambridge University and he had begun a fund raisingfund raising campaign. Among the other requests he made was a proposal to Lady Margaret Beaufort, the mother-in-law of Henry VIII. He asked her to subsidize the Lady Margaret Professor of Divinity at Cambridge. She agreed, but also decided to pay for a similar chair at Oxford. Of course, that original subsidy needed to be upgraded with the financial changes of centuries. By the time Macquarie assumed the office, there was a house on the Christ Church College quad provided for him and his family in addition to a salary and benefits. No longer did this include a full staff of servants and horses and carriages of the sixteenth century. But it was quite satisfying in other ways. I had the privilege of dining with Macquarrie and his wife in their Christ Church College quarters and admired the durability of Lady Margaret's long standing contribution. Macquarie supplemented his income with his popular books and prosperous lecture invitations.

One story I recall from the dinner conversation about one of my favorite authors, William Barclay. He was famous for his enormously popular scripture commentaries on the four Gospels. Even to this day, thousands of ministers and priests often consult Barclay for his careful reconstruction of Gospel scenes based on fascinating studies of the folk customs and culture of the Palestine of Christ's day. He conveys clear insight into Christ's teachings, sermons and dialogues with the Pharisees. Barclay has a remarkable ability to draw applications from the texts to our spiritual and moral lives. Bishop Sheen was once asked what scripture scholar he would recommend and he replied immediately: "Use William Barclay."

It turned out that Macquarrie, as a young minister, was assigned as an assistant to Barclay in Glasgow, Scotland. He noticed that Barclay spent hour upon noisy hour at his typewriter, driven by something. Barcley told Macquarrie:

> I asked Dr. Barclay about his deep dedication to writing. He told me that, some years ago, a tragedy followed the marriage of his daughter and her husband. On their honeymoon, the couple sailed into a storm in the Irish channel. The boat sank and they drowned. He went on to say, "My grief has been so great at times that I need to plunge myself in hard work to be able to survive. However, though God did not still the waters of the sea for them, he has stilled the storm in my soul and that of my wife so we could go on."

Cardinal Suenens' Oxford Mission

With the arrival of spring and a burst of yellow daffo-
dils, the Belgian Cardinal Suenens, a principal partici-
pant in the proceedings of the second Vatican Council,
ardent member of the charismatic renewal movement
and gifted proponent of ecumenism arrived to conduct
the University Mission, the first Catholic to do so since
the Reformation. The theme of his mission was "My God
and Yours." For one week he delivered a mission sermon
each evening in the Sheldonian Theater.*

Besides his nightly sermons, Suenens visited the
numerous colleges and drew groups of students to sit
and discuss their notions of God. It was quite popular.
During my Lumen Vitae days, I had seen Suenens several
times and had participated in his liturgies in Brussels.
The members of the university, wearing their colorful
academic robes, attended his final sermon. What I recall
most from that service was the singing of the magnificent
hymn to the Holy Spirit, "Come down, O love divine,

---

* Built in 1664–8 the Sheldonian Theater was commissioned by
Gilbert Sheldon, Archbishop of Canterbury and designed by Sir
Christopher Wren who was asked to follow a plan of an ancient
Roman sports arena and avoid having pillars to support the roof.
Wren achieved this ideal by importing tall oak trees from Ireland
and using an intricate balancing of the long trunks crossing each
other and sustained by the walls. The reason for the theater was
in response to the local churches that wanted secular gatherings
have their own structure. Nonetheless, Cardinal Suenens' religious Mission was held at the Sheldonian, doubtless to accommodate the standing room only crowds.

seek now this soul of mine, and visit it with your own ardor glowing." During Suenens' visit, it certainly seemed that ardor of the Holy Spirit was glowing.

During my time at Oxford, I was impressed by the highest standards of education and also the residue of Christianity, both Catholic and High Anglican. I was impressed that the university chose a Catholic cardinal for their retreat and still relish the judgment of a Don who said that Suenens was the greatest retreat master since the Anglican Archbishop Temple in the 1930s.

I found that the University sponsors summer seminars on Cardinal Newman, which Monsignor Kelly and I attended for two summers. I also discovered that, every four years, Oxford hosts a seminar on the Fathers of the Church, two sessions of which I attended with Monsignor Kelly. I am now able to appreciate Newman's wonderful contributions to our faith, almost a Church Father himself and also canonized by Pope Benedict, an occasion which Monsignor Kelly and I attended. The effect of these Oxford experiences was, mainly, to challenge me to never stop studying the history of the Church, ever ancient, ever new. The experience deepened my faith, which helped me to be more ardent in sharing the faith with the teachers served by NCEA.

Planning NCEA Conventions

Another responsibility that came my way was planning the religious education part of the annual NCEA

Convention, which was held every year during Easter week. We always drew good attendance and had some great guests over the years, including Mother Teresa and Ronald Reagan. For a number of years after I retired from NCEA, Msgr. Jack Meyers invited me to give the closing talk at a convention, usually after one or other American president who was sure to appeal to a full house. This also meant that weary convention goers were, by this time, tired out and headed for home, so I had a humbler size audience which was fine by me. One year, however, Jack gave me the slot before the main speaker. That year, it was Ronald Reagan. The hall at the Hilton hotel on Connecticut Avenue in Washington DC, seated seven thousand people, and it was packed.

Everyone had to pass through a metal detector to get in. I used the president's podium, though his seal was not yet attached to it. Despite their weariness, the audience was lively, receptive to my corny jokes, and attentive to my thoughts about ten future trends in Catholic education. With five minutes to go, a stream of TV news leaders, Dan Rather, Katie Couric, Britt Hume, and Dianne Sawyer, as well as editors from the *New York Times* and *Washington Post* passed in front of me as I spoke. I ad-libbed, "I am impressed that the cream of the media came all the way here to listen to the value of Catholic education," to the amusement of the crowd and their applause, at which I ended. Reagan greeted each of us on stage while his seal was applied to the podium. A week later, I received an autographed picture of the President with me seated with others on the stage.

Retirement from NCEA

In 1979 I realized that I was only a year away from my fiftieth birthday. After fifteen years in Washington, I told Jack Meyers that I was ready to go home. After the excitement of my Catholic University years and the constant travel and change associated with my marvelous years at the NCEA, I knew I now needed the quiet and spiritual renewal that St. Norbert Abbey could provide. I participated in the search for a successor, and, after a number of interviews, I decided to meet with Father Francis Kelly to try to convince him to take the post. He looked interested, but knew that he would have to pray over it and clear it with Bishop Flanagan in Worcester.

It took several months, a number of ups and downs along with near acceptance and constant delays before a decision was made. Eventually Fr. Kelly received the permission of his bishop and agreed to accept the post with the approval of the NCEA staff and the board. He became an excellent leader of the Religious Education at NCEA for the next thirteen years, during which he became an admired national leader in the field and in the American Church.

I had just celebrated my silver jubilee as a priest and was ready to go home and be a born again into the Norbertine community. With all my heart I thank

Monsignor Jack Meyers, Monsignor Frank Barrett, Nancy Brewer, Rhoda Goldstein, Isabella, Joe O'Donnell, and all the staff at NCEA who patiently taught me how to function in a National Catholic office and trained me to witness Christ and his Church in the ministry of Catholic education.

CHAPTER FOURTEEN

Home Again at St. Norbert's

It is therefore by her conduct and her life that the Church will evangelize the world. In other words the Church does this by her living witness of fidelity to the Lord Jesus—the witness of poverty and detachment, of freedom in the face of the powers of this world, the witness of sanctity.

—Pope Paul VI, "On Evangelization," 41

St. Norbert admonishes us: "Without organization and without a rule, and without the instructions of the Fathers, it is impossible to fulfill the apostolic and evangelical mandates. Such assistance is offered to us in the Rule of St. Augustine and the Constitutions of the Order of Premontré whereby we are inspired and directed in conforming our lives to Christ's Gospel and the apostolic preaching."

—Day of Pentecost—Constitutions, 50

I was given little time to settle back into Abbey life before Abbot Tremel appointed me to be a planner for the

community. Since it was a new position, I was starting
from scratch. The abbot placed me on his council as well
as the boards of our college and two high schools. I had
regularly attended our annual chapter meetings which
provided me with a general outline of our progress and
challenges. I had also stayed in touch with my closest
friends in the community who helped me be aware of
our situation and understand some developments.

At the start of my work as a planner, I noted that certain decisions had already been made. We had returned
the parishes we had been serving for many years in
Montana and in the peninsula north of Green Bay to their
respective dioceses. We retained our four parishes in De
Pere, Green Bay, and Bay Settlement. Despite returning
some parishes, we expanded our outreach by opening a
mission in Lima, Peru. Pope John XXIII had encouraged
religious communities in the United States to help Latin
America with missionaries who would sustain the faith
during the difficult times facing them. We opened the
parish of San Norberto in Lima that was soon prospering
under our care. However, our men wanted to be closer to
the poorest of the poor and eventually received a mission
in San Juan Lurigancho.

During my term, I visited them in Lurigancho and
was inspired by their joy in serving people who needed
hope and confidence. Most of their homes were like tents
made of tin. Many of them had stacked small piles of
bricks by their doors, which they planned to use to build
walls. The dirt streets became mud in rainy seasons.

Drinking water was supplied by tank trucks that brought it around regularly. Yet, despite their poverty, the villagers dressed with dignity for Sunday Mass. Our men lived very simply and felt very close to their people. Their witness of faith and concern for their people was contagious. I suggested that they consider recruiting vocations with the possibility of establishing a foundation. Father Strenski eventually began this apostolate. In the meantime they built a beautiful church. Since then, that whole area has been transformed into a middle class neighborhood with paved streets, an integrated water supply, and electricity.

Not long after our arrival in Lurigancho, our community approved Father Jack McCarthy's request to open yet another mission in Santa Clotilde on the Napo River in northeastern Peru. The village is only accessible by a ten-hour boat ride from Iquitos, the nearest city. Father Jack had become a medical doctor and was joined by another priest doctor, Father Maurice Schroeder, O.M.I., from Canada. Father Lambert Baeten arrived to serve as pastor for the parish that extended miles along the river. As of this writing, Father McCarthy is in his twenty-fifth year serving his riverside mission.

After many years of service, Fr. Lambert's good heart gave out and by his own wishes was buried with his people. Jack also had several health scares. One of them was so serious that a sea-plane came to rescue him. All his worried people gathered to watch him leave and send him off with love and prayers and anxiety as they watched him go into the skies—perhaps forever. He survived and returned to give more of his life to them.

Pennings (St. Norbert) High School

While the mission in Peru was exciting, and doing a lot of great work, much of my time as a planner was directed to our high schools and college. We still had a number of Norbertines on staff at each of them. Pennings, originally St. Norbert High School, had the longest track record in our community. Founded by Abbot Pennings, it was often overshadowed by the college which he also founded. I came to the promising situation of a school that appeared ready for an independent identity and to be financially secure.

Norbertine Father Jackson Feldman describes the school I saw at this point:

> At this moment it finally had its own building—a former public high school—with its own labs for biology, chemistry and physics as well as a cafeteria. A music department with band and chorus was introduced. Also a small gymnasium, an auditorium with a stage for theater and concerts. A chapel for daily Mass and for reservation of the Blessed Sacrament was located in the center of the building . . . Parental involvement grew tremendously to the point where administration and teachers, parents, students, staff and alumni became in very fact the 'Pennings Family.' On

this date September 1980, Norbertine Father
Gery Meehan became the principal of the school
for the next eleven years.

(From a self-published Norbertine book,
With the Grace of God, page 81)

I had taught at this school when I was a seminarian
and had an emotional attachment. The future looked
reasonably bright, but it ended up closing eleven years
later. That year the basketball team won the state Catholic
championship and the high school choir gave a concert
at Carnegie Hall in New York City. It was the little school
that could. Father Feldman cited a student's comment in
the school newspaper: "Everybody tells us that Pennings
is closing, but nobody tells us why." Feldman concluded:
"That last graduation was held on June 1, 1990. That
night, a light went out in De Pere, forever." (p. 81)

St. Norbert College—Growing Pains

I found St. Norbert College humming along relatively
well. President Neil Webb was working on a policy to cap
enrollment while increasing the number of applications,
thus assuring a higher-quality student body. That ideal
was adopted in a limited way by succeeding presidents,
and today Dr. Webb's academic hopes are being fulfilled.
Moreover, the campus is beautiful with abundant trees
and bushes and lawns provide a park-like appearance,
dotted with colonial-style, red brick buildings, clean,
solid, and well kept.

The issue that engaged my attention as planner was Abbot Tremel's plan to separately incorporate the College from the Premonstratarian Order. As the college grew, so also did its finances and potential of serious debt that might prove a threat to the Order. The Abbot did not want that debt to be a threat to the stability of the Order. I worked with our Finance manager, Father Robert Finnegan, to develop the process that would bring this about.

We worked in constant contact with President Webb, who was generous in giving us his time and in cooperating with the proposal. Other Catholic colleges and universities had already completed this process with success.

Father Robert and I flew to Denver to meet an expert in this matter. He stressed the need for our Order to adopt a number of reserved powers, some of which dealt with limits on borrowing by the college. He also stressed the importance of maintaining the Catholic identity of the college, such as hiring a Catholic president who would support our efforts. At the time the worry about Catholic identity did not seem worrisome.

We had a strong tradition of Catholic influence from our Norbertine presence on the faculty along with our lay professors and a lively majority of our students were Catholic. I believed, at the time, we had sufficient reserved powers to support its Catholic identity. At this time, we also created a new board of trustees that had a significant number of Norbertines on it. In fact, I later served two five-year terms on that board. Some years later, Norbertine Father Dane Radecki sponsored the creation of an office for Mission and Heritage, designed to support the college's Catholic identity within the tradition of the Norbertine Order. I gratefully report that the college awarded me an honorary doctorate, an alumni award and an award from the department of Education.

On Maryhill Drive
Premontré Becomes Notre Dame de la Baie

We sponsored another high school in Green Bay: Premontré, named after the first Abbey founded by St. Norbert in 1121. The Abbey financed the building of a handsome school with an auditorium, a gym, a chapel, and a priory for the Norbertine teachers. There was also a football field with bleachers and room for parking. The school opened in autumn 1959, the same year that the new St. Norbert Abbey opened. The year the school opened, it welcomed 848 boys. Twenty Norbertine teachers and a staff of experienced lay teachers ensured a smooth transition from its former existence as Central Catholic High School in downtown Green Bay.

By 1980, when I joined their board there were 589 boys, and fifteen Norbertines were still on hand to maintain the Order's ideals and religious influence. Sports of all kinds thrived at the school. Football was king but there were successes with basketball, hockey, golf, and tennis. Its most unique successes occurred on the stage where

Father Guyon produced one musical hit after another. In some respects, the annual musical was the highlight of the year. The widespread involvement of students, faculty, and staff was phenomenal.

But during my time on the board questions about finances and the future began to arise. I recall from the NCEA days that a high school is something like a smaller version of a college. It needs tuition that covers a certain percentage of the costs, annual fund raising, and an ever-increasing foundation to bolster funds for future growth and needs. And, besides this, a Catholic school should provide scholarships for needy students. Premontré was, in many ways, thriving, but enrollment was down, and it seemed clear that at some point, it would no longer be sustainable.

Nine years later, Norbertine Father Dane Radecki became principal and presided over the transformation of Premontré. It merged with Pennings and St. Joseph Academy for girls to become a coed school called Notre Dame de la Baie. The new school, sponsored by the Green Bay Diocese, has survived and is steadily growing.

Our Inner Life

By 1980, sad to say, the Church in the United States was undergoing a crisis of vocations. The shortage led to the closing of many Catholic elementary and secondary schools and the decline of parish ministry by male religious. This was discussed at our annual chapters during my four years as planner. One response was the writing of a Mission statement to sharpen our goals and practices. Useful Church documents were available such as Vatican II documents on the liturgy, the Church, the priesthood, and religious life. Male and female religious orders established new societies that met regularly to deal with the crisis. In those first years there was some optimism and hope for the future. However, along with most others, we seemed spellbound. The old saying was true: "It takes a long time to turn the Queen Mary around."

During these years, many articles and books were published, citing what they believed to be the causes of, and offering occasional solutions to, the unwelcome crisis that affected the Church in Western Europe, Canada, and the United States. I thought at the time that we were too close to the problem to know how to address it. Worse yet the tragic explosion of the sex abuse news by the clergy virtually paralyzed for a time a Church that was already being pummeled by the media. In the middle of the chaos, I came across a teaching of scripture while praying the Liturgy of the Hours that powerfully described a situation parallel to ours. It contained within it what our response should be, though it would be difficult. The text is from the wisdom of the Canticle of Habbakuk, who, three thousand years ago, faced crisis and chaos and a challenge to his faith:

> For though the fig tree blossom not,
>   nor fruit be on the vines,

Though the yield of the olive fail,
    and the terraces produce no nourishment.

Though the flocks disappear from the fold
    and there be no herd in the stalls,

Yet will I rejoice in the Lord
    and exult in my saving God!

God, my Lord is my strength!
    He makes my feet swift as those of hinds
    and enables me to go upon the heights.

(Canticle of Habakkuk, 3:17–19)

This is good advice and a model of a faith response to life's troubles. I found even more insight from Psalm 44. The psalmist reminds God that he has been a faithful servant in spite of the troubles he faces:

All this has come upon us though we had not
    forgotten you, nor have we been false to your
    covenant;

Our hearts have not shrunk back,
    nor our steps turned aside from your path.

I liked the boldness of his intercessory prayer that followed:

Awake! Why are you asleep, O Lord?

Arise! Cast us not off forever!

Why do you hide your face, forgetting our woe
    and oppression?

Arise! Help us! Redeem us for your kindness'
    sake.

               (Ps 44:18–19; 24–5, 27)

In my next assignment I would really need Habakkuk's wisdom and the holy boldness of the singer of Psalm 44.

CHAPTER 15

The Albuquerque Mission

THE Franciscan Sisters of Colorado Springs sponsored a fruitful hospital mission for over a hundred
years. Some years before World War II, they had a surplus of vocations and responded to an invitation from the
archdiocese of Santa Fe, New Mexico, to staff some new
elementary schools. They also opened a small college in
Albuquerque for their sisters so they could be trained
as teachers. They named it St. Joseph's College on the
Rio Grande. As it grew, other young women applied for
entrance into their department of education.

Over the years, the college grew and the Sisters
eventually expanded it and renamed it The University
of Albuquerque. But like most religious communities,
the vocations to the Sisters eventually declined and they
needed to replace the administration and staff with laity
which strained their finances. Their first lay presidents
did well but did not stay for lengthy tenures, which was
needed for stability. Gradually the Sisters had to finance
the school beyond their means. They considered selling
the university.

However, complaints were sent to the office of the
Apostolic Delegate of the Vatican in Washington, DC,

opposing the sale and citing the Church's rule forbidding "alienation of Church property." Someone, who probably knew me from NCEA, proposed that I should be asked to be appointed president of the university. I received a letter from Archbishop Sanchez inviting me to come for an interview to discuss the possibility. With Abbot Mackin's approval, I accepted the interview.

I met with the archbishop, the university's chairman of the board, and Sister Stephanie McReynolds who represented the Sisters. Our meeting was friendly and they made me feel welcome. Sister Stephanie said that I should plan to turn the university over to the archdiocese. The Archbishop agreed to study this offer. Two years later this plan was fulfilled and the archdiocese took over the university.

Discussions about my appointment were discussed by the Abbot and Council and, finally, it was agreed I should accept their offer. My first day in office should have let me know I would have four rough years in this task. I opened a letter from my predecessor. In broad terms, he wrote that the best way to save the university was to eliminate the liberal arts and religion departments, and turn the place into a business college. That would be a success. He was probably right, but that was opposed to our identity as a Catholic liberal arts school and simply out of the question. It was a small school with about a thousand students on campus and five hundred night school students from Kirkland Air Force Base. The majority of students were Hispanic and Native Americans who relied on federal subsidies for tuition and other expenses. The faculty welcomed me and trusted that I could save the school. I thought so too, but it was not to be.

I asked Abbot Mackin if I could have Father Bob Brooks as the university chaplain and a sociology professor and Father Bob Olson for a religion professor and these requests were granted. The first two years went reasonably well. The board elected Gina McKee as the chairwoman and she became a tower of strength for me. The board was used to being involved in the school's future and I was impressed with their commitment. I recall one member telling me that, "We don't leave our brains at the door." I was invited to join the Economic Forum, a group of the leaders of education, industry, finance, and business. They met once a month for breakfast and talked shop. Several became close friends and made significant financial contributions to the school.

Father Brooks had already been appointed to scout for a new foundation for ministry to Hispanics. I encouraged him to choose Albuquerque which was at least 50 percent Hispanic and a promising ground for such a mission. Eventually this proposal was accepted and with the leadership of Father Joel Garner a community was established that survived a number of challenges but has finally become a Norbertine Abbey with Fr. Joel as Abbot.

The university provided a house for me near Old Town where San Felipe de Neri Church and parish was situated. For more than three hundred years, this church has been has been the spiritual heart of Albuquerque.

That heart is still beating strong, offering liturgical, pastoral, and educational services to parishioners and visitors. The present church building, constructed in 1793, is
listed on the National Register of Historic Places.

In my first weeks, I regularly found a freshly baked
loaf of bread wrapped in tin foil at my door. Eventually
someone told me that it was a gift of Eleanor Lopez who
lived around the corner with her husband Joe. He and
Eleanor reached out to me to offer their friendship and
support for the university. I also received the hospitality
of their children and families, especially Owen and Vicki,
Tim and Rhonda, and Cathy.

Gradually, I came to know the staff, faculty, students,
and a growing number of the pastors, as well as culture
of the city which prided itself on its Hispanic and Native
American history. Each August, the convention center
hosted the week long Feria Artesana featuring original
works by New Mexican artists. I purchased an original
wood-carved eighteen-inch-tall Madonna and Child
that I still have on my desk. It is titled, *Maria Santissima*
(Most Holy Mary) carved by the distinguished *santero*,
Max Roybal. In New Mexico, saint-making or *santero* is
a devotional practice that tells the story of Catholic saints
through *retablos*, panel paintings of saints, and *bultos*,
hand-carved statues of saints.

The statue became part of one of my first efforts to
make the university more widely known in New Mexico.
I met with the head of a local TV station that broadcast
across the state to discuss the possibility of having a TV

Mass sponsored by the university. It was my good luck that an evangelical program from Ohio was about to terminate its contract for their Sunday half hour service at 8:00 a.m. The director of the station offered me a three-year contract for a set fee. I was convinced that I would receive enough donations to pay for it without having to add to the school's budget. After Communion I pointed to the statue of Mary that I had purchased and prayed for her intercession on behalf of the home-bound audience who made up the biggest portion of the followers. I asked for donations to sustain the broadcast

Blessed Mary helped a lot: donations for the next three years always paid the bill with a small surplus for the school. Letters poured in with donations. I recall several from elderly home-bound couples who wrote that they loved the Mass and always dressed in their Sunday best to attend it on TV. I believed this would assure a better understanding of the university as a Catholic one despite its secular name. (The name of St. Joseph's College on the Rio Grande would have been a far better brand name.)

It turned out that my business manager was a Mormon. He was a capable staff member and patiently explained to me the financial setup during a weekly meeting. The news was not good. There was no endowment and there was very little in reserve and the debt payments needed to be met. The staff had to reconstruct the alumni names and addresses. Annual giving was low. We were in trouble.

In my second year, my business manager invited

me to Sunday morning services at their Mormon Ward church the equivalent of what we call a parish church. The meeting place was a hall and the service included readings and comments and a message on a screen from the head of the Mormon church in Salt lake City. The community was family oriented with lots of young people and children. That sunny, typically New Mexican day there was a picnic with all the festivities. It was a pleasant visit and I enjoyed seeing something of the religious activities of the Mormons. I admired their practice of calling their young men to do evangelizing ministry full time for at least two years before they begin their professional careers, not just in the United States but also in other countries.

The Final Crisis

By my third year, the finances were in deep crisis. I joined Archbishop Sanchez, his lawyer, an economic adviser, and our board chairwoman for a meeting with the board of the bank to discuss getting another loan. They refused. Afterwards I met with the Archbishop who said that we may need to close the university. I had been active in fund raising, but it was not nearly enough. I asked him to consider one more year in which we would hire a professional firm to conduct a fund raising campaign. He must have been considering this himself because he quickly agreed.

The campaign lasted from the beginning of my third year in office to the middle of the fourth. We did acquire substantial pledges, and there were amusing moments. I recall making a pitch to a Methodist couple who said, "Don't you think it's crazy to want Methodists to support a Catholic school?" I replied, "Yes, well there is a Methodist in my madness." In another case a prospective donor said, "You have a five-million-dollar baby. Find that money and you will survive." And I stretched out my hand and said, "Would you like to give us the baby?" He just laughed.

While there were a number of bright spots and positive moments, it soon became clear that it was too little and too late. One night, I was alone at home, and became fully aware and overwhelmed by the outcome. Spontaneously, I knelt on the floor and begged God to get me and all concerned through this. By the beginning of the second semester of my fourth year as president I had to announce the closing of the school. The last graduation would take place in June. The University of New Mexico volunteered to store the student records. There was anger and disappointment and several student protests. I did what I could to make the best of a bad situation. We were able to relocate all students to other colleges, especially the University of New Mexico and Christian Brothers College of Santa Fe whose president, Brother Donald Mouton, was a good friend and counselor for me. I also owed a great deal to Gina McKee and the members of the board for their strong support throughout this painful process. They discussed and argued all the details at length and finally voted for the closing of the university.

Gina's husband, Lloyd, who ran an automobile business, was also a friend during my time of need.

With the school set to close, one more tragedy occurred just before graduation. A young man shot his girlfriend in the back as she tried to run away from him before turning the gun on himself. When I arrived on the scene, they were on the floor in the corridor. I made an attempt to speak with each of them but received no response. While I prayed for them, the medics came in and air-lifted them to the hospital, where they soon died. I recall with gratitude the head of the nursing school told me that she and a partner would meet with each student to help them cope with the tragedy. I called the archbishop and each board member to tell them what happened.

I failed a lot of very good and admirable people in Albuquerque and I acknowledge that with grief and hope for forgiveness.

Despite the dismay, the graduation ceremony went on with traditional dignity and form. That summer, there were details of all kinds that needed attention. The archdiocese was now in charge of the property and was in a position to move St. Pius X High School from downtown Albuquerque to the campus after sufficient adaptations were made. Parents on the east side resisted the change, but in time the transfer worked and where a failing college had stood, a very successful Catholic High school is flourishing. What was once the administration building for the university is now the chancery for the archdiocese of Santa Fe. The gift to Albuquerque by the Franciscan

Sisters of Colorado Springs lives on in new and vital form of Catholic education. I thank them, especially Sister Stephanie McReynolds, for giving me the privilege of trying to save the school which, alas, I was unable to do.

I remember with gratitude the strength and understanding I received from Archbishop Sanchez throughout my tenure at the university and during the days of the final crisis. With his leadership, the archdiocese did whatever they could to sustain the school. Their resources were slim, since the largest part of their congregations were poor and working-class Hispanics, many of whom were and are recently arrived immigrants. The Church in Albuquerque was dynamic in serving the poor and showed a spirit of a missionary enthusiasm and that indeed was their top priority. Sanchez was as loved as any bishop could ever hope and I was the beneficiary of his thoughtfulness throughout my own troubles. He was a Good Shepherd for me. I mourn the misfortunes that he himself had to endure later and will not rehearse them here. In his own sorrow he acted humbly and bore the pain with dignity. He has passed away. I pray for him with a tribute popular with Boston priests, "Archbishop Sanchez, may God be good to you."

I have one other story from those days I wish to share. One of our Norbertine priests, Father Ed Sdano, came to Albuquerque to join our new foundation and served as pastor of Holy Rosary parish entrusted to our care. He was young and looked healthy, but he had inherited heart trouble. He joined a pilgrimage for priestly vocations to what is called the "Lourdes of America," the Sanctuary of Chimayo. The strain was too much for him and he suffered a fatal heart attack a day later. At the funeral, a squadron of men chanted three salutes: *Viva Cristo Rey! Viva La Virgen Maria!* And, with, deep affection, *Viva Padre Eduardo!* (Long live Christ the King! Long live our Virgin Mary! Long live father Edward!) Amen. It was an illustration of the ardent faith of many of the people of New Mexico. Despite my failure to save the university, I am grateful to have spent time among these faith-filled people.

CHAPTER 16

_____

Invitation: The Search for God, Self and Church

A Catholic Learning Guide for Adults

A NOTHER friend that God sent into my life was the legendary Paulist Father Alvin Illig. He deserves the credit for recovering for Catholics their mission of evangelization. He encouraged me to write a Catechism for adults in RCIA (Rite of Christian Initiation of Adults) He wanted the book to be called Invitation and, subsequently, published it through his office for evangelization in 1984.

I subsequently revised the text in 1994 to reflect the guidance of the new Catechism of the Catholic Church. I also revised it again in 2006 to include the direction of the American Bishops' Adult Catechism.

Invitation is one of the four most popular of my many books,* staying in print through three editions since 1984. Its appeal is partly due to a question and answer approach with extensive answers to each question. I have tried to

_____

* The other three are *Essentials of the Faith* and *The Teen Catechism* (Our Sunday Visitor Press) and *The Story of the Church* (Franciscan Media).

be pastoral throughout the text so that it is a Catechism focused on the personal growth of the reader. Since it is mainly used by converts to the Catholic Church. It meets their needs on their journey of faith and it is also deeply based on scripture.

CHAPTER 17

Preparing for the 1987 Papal Visit

O N a languid day in July of that summer, I received a letter from Father Tom Gallagher, head of the department of Catholic education at the Bishops' Conference building in Washington DC He invited me to come to the capitol city for a meeting to discuss what religious educators could do to help prepare for the second pastoral visit of Pope John Paul II to the United States. I felt God was once again looking out for me and leading me to another way to serve him.

About fifteen national leaders of religious education for both schools and parish-based programs were present. I knew most of them and enjoyed seeing them again. The discussions that followed wandered in all directions and the participants seemed unable to settle down and begin to offer concrete advice. As a veteran of such gatherings I was not surprised at the vagueness of the members and the need to make a "three-point-landing," as pilots used to say.

After lunch, I decided to push for practical suggestions. I used a healthy dose of Irish guilt to get things moving, such as pointing out the expense of bringing us here and the cost of our hotel rooms. We should not waste time and money. It was our responsibility to help the Church in the United States to offer applications to the religious education of our people that would be stimulated by the personal inspiration of Pope John Paul. The excitement for the faith his visit would foster among hundreds of thousands participants in ten cities would be a blessing for the Church. If there ever was a teaching moment, this was clearly one made in heaven for the benefit of earth.

The tactic worked and the rest of the afternoon flowed beautifully with plenty of useful ideas for religious education that could benefit from the papal visit. The group praised the scriptural text that was adopted as a sort of keynote for the visit. The words set the tone and goal for the occasion:

> And he gave some as apostles, others as prophets, others as evangelists, others as pastors and teachers to build up the body of Christ, until we all attain to the unity of faith and knowledge of the Son of God, to mature manhood, to the extent of the full stature of Christ.
>
> (Eph 4:11–13)

Soon after my return west, I received a letter from Father Gallagher to come back to Washington to work at the Bishops' Conference for one year while writing the catechesis, based on the Ephesus text, that would accompany the papal visit. With Abbot Mackin's approval, I accepted the invitation. I was given an office in the

Conference building and was provided living quarters in the Bishops' staff house in Northeast Washington not far from the Catholic University campus and next door to the Franciscan monastery and their popular Shrine of the Holy Land that has replicas of scenes from the Holy Land. I lived across the hall from Father Robert (Bob) Lynch who was first assistant to the Secretary General of the Bishops' Conference, Monsignor Daniel Hoye.

I had met Father Lynch during my NCEA days in Washington. He was very helpful in guiding me through the details I needed for working at the Conference, and he was a good friend at the staff house. In fact, as I labored over the catechesis with my typewriter, he introduced me to the wonders of the computers which were beginning to become popular. With his guidance, to my satisfaction, I obtained my first computer and never looked back. What a blessing! I was also introduced to a layman, Paul Etienne, who had been in seminary and was now part of the team preparing for the visit.

The community of priests at the staff house represented a profile of the national services sponsored by the bishops to the Church in the United States. I have always liked community life as I knew it from the Norbertines, and, now experienced a similar community life and spirit there. The chapel, where we recited Morning and Evening Prayer and concelebrated Mass, had just been renovated in a medieval style with marble and statues from an Italian company that specialized in reproducing beautiful and sacred medieval art.

The papal visit was scheduled for September through October 1987. Towards the end of that summer, I received the good news that I would be part of the visit, as a representative of the Bishops to the media. I was expected to be present in the hall where the media were situated. Mainly I would be open to answer any questions they might have about the Church, its teachings, the meaning of the pope's addresses, or Catholic customs they did not understand or know anything about.

When the time came to join the trip we flew to Miami where the Pope would begin his pastoral visit. I met a driver at 5:30 a.m. the next morning, who took me to my first assignment: to be a guest on the *Today Show*.

When we arrived at the "studio," a large flatbed trailer, I saw no one. Finally, a man approached me. He introduced himself, but I don't recall his telling me whom he represented. He asked me, "Have you ever been on the *Today Show* or on a papal visit?" I said, "No." He proceeded to train me. "You will be one of two guests. The other guest will be a representative from the State government in Florida. I would advise you to be a good listener and avoid controversy. May I ask you what you might say if you he asks you reply to the complaint that it is not right to use so much taxpayer money to pay for a religious event?" I was stumped from the start. My interviewer went on to supply me with an answer that worked. "The people, who come to see the Pope, have a right to see him and a right to be safe in the process. Taxes include funds that protect people attending large public events whether religious or otherwise." He gave me a few more questions with suggested replies but I don't recall them. I was a bit numb yet with the travel and early morning duties.

He seemed to disappear as quickly as he arrived. I began thinking of him as an angel sent to launch me on the trip, though the truth probably was that he came from the archdiocesan office in downtown Miami. Before I knew it, Bryant Gumbel, the veteran host of the *Today Show* in those days, came on the air with greetings and questions. The interview was over in ten minutes just in time for an ad. The interview went well, and I answered the tax question just as my angel had instructed me. A good start.

I returned to the hotel and proceeded to the press room. The TV sets showed the greeting ceremony at the Miami airport upon the arrival of Pope John Paul. From there, the pope traveled to St. Martha's parish for the preliminary ceremonies of greeting. Papal custom called for beginning such visits with clergy. There were snipers on the roofs along the pope's route, and the streets were emptied because of the fear that remained after the pope's near-assassination several years earlier.

Normally there would only be one lecture given by the pope. This visit changed that approach by having someone address the pope first. It was thought that such a dialogue would make the experience richer and more compelling for all concerned. The throng of priests in the church had representatives from all the dioceses of the United States. The priest elected to give the speech to the pope was Father Frank McNulty from the Newark archdiocese. He was the favorite of the progressive clergy at a time when Pope John Paul was leading the Church toward a more conservative goal.

Father McNulty was an engaging and famous story-teller, and he lived up to that reputation with his opening story. He spoke of a banquet in England held in one of the many stately homes in the British countryside. The guest of honor for the evening was a popular Shakespearean actor. At the end of the meal the host invited the actor to recite some well-known soliloquies from the Bard's plays. The actor complied and was greeted with extended applause. Then the host added, "Would you recite the Shepherd psalm?" He replied, "I will do so if Father Brown will recite the psalm after me."

The proposal was accepted. The actor delivered the psalm with his customary dramatic talent and bowed as the delighted guests applauded. Father Brown rose and head down and with a quiet voice he spoke the words of the psalm with so much personal faith and love for the beauty of the words that when he finished, the listeners were hushed into silence. The actor arose and said, "Did you see what happened tonight? When I recited the psalm you cheered. When Father Brown spoke you remained silent in prayer. What does this mean? It means I knew the psalm. It means Father Brown knew the Shepherd."

Father McNulty then stressed the need to foster a priesthood that was deeply in love with Jesus in an evident and personal way. Among the several points he made there was a plea to consider exploring again the vow of celibacy in the Western Church. Pope John Paul's first line in his response was one that an Irishman could appreciate, "Father McNulty, 'It's a long road to Tipperary.'" The pope then proceeded to deliver his challenge to priests to live up to the training and ideals they received in seminary and the vows they made at ordination.

After following both talks on TV, I was approached by Joel Berger, a columnist for the *New York Times*. He reviewed several items from the pope's speech and asked me what they meant. The material was familiar to me and I offered him my interpretation of the talk. This was my first test case in dealing with reporters on this trip. An hour later, Joel returned with his article wondering if he was being fair to the meaning of the pope's words. I was delighted he asked me and happier yet to praise him for his accuracy in his article. The next morning, the first thing I did was read the article. I was relieved to find that Joel's report contained the interpretations I had given him. Generally, I had similar experiences with the other reporters and was relieved that the pope was getting a fair interpretation of his words. Of course, in their editorials they often disagreed with Pope John Paul, but at least most of them reported his words accurately.

I was blessed to be assigned with Paul Etienne as a seat mate as we traveled by plane to the various cities on the pope's agenda. Paul and I had lots of time to get to know each other. Born and raised in Indiana, he had two brothers who were priests and a sister who was a nun. He himself had been a seminarian. I wondered if he was reconsidering a return to seminary. He did go back, and was ordained a few years later. I was privileged to attend his ordination, First Mass, and the feasting. He has since become the bishop of Cheyenne, Wyoming, where I had the honor to be present at his installation as bishop.

A pope in the middle of the Bible Belt

We landed in Columbia, SC, on the second afternoon of the papal visit. Our bus took us to the stadium on the campus of the University of South Carolina for an ecumenical celebration. The pope met with the leaders of Protestant faiths where formal speeches were made and prayers for Christian unity recited. Seventy-thousand people crowded the stadium and I had a birds-eye view of it all from a press box.

The event began with a procession of thirty leaders of various Protestant faith communities dressed in their unique robes. As I watched them I felt I was watching the thread of church history chronicling centuries of departure from Catholicism. All of the anger and fire of revolution that lurked in their backgrounds were tempered by time and wisdom and even illumined by the respect they were paying to Pope John Paul II during his visit. The crowd applauded them.

Due to a complaint, no Cross could be planted on state property until the pope actually arrived. The objection seemed silly since the majority of the audience were fervent Southern Baptists in a state with a small body of Catholics. The Baptists certainly had no problem with a Cross. The solution to the dilemma was ingenious. As the pope's appearance was announced and the crowd stood, the music for the glorious hymn, "When I Survey the Wondrous Cross," began. From the left end zone, college boys in jeans and bare feet emerged carrying a large Cross in a horizontal position. At the same time, from the near side college girls in jeans and bare feet carried a huge tapestry of "The Lamb Slain and Risen." Think of that as these words escorted them:

> When I survey the wondrous Cross
> On which the king of glory died.
> My richest gain I count but loss
> And pour contempt on all my pride.

As that stately procession moved toward the other end zone, the fervor of the music and faith of 70,000 voices mounted with a kind ecstasy I have rarely experienced:

> See from his head, his hands, his feet
> How love and grief flow mingling down
> Did 'ere such love and sorrow meet
> Or thorns compose so rich a crown.

When the procession arrived at its destination, the Cross of Christ was mounted on State University earth and the tapestry of the Lamb of God was unfolded over the grass usually trod by football players. At that precise moment Pope John Paul II appeared. After the applause the final stanza was sung.

> Were the whole realm of nature mine,
>   That were a present far too small,
> Love so amazing, so divine,
>   Demands my life, my love, my all.

Among the pope's many inspiring words to the people in the stadium these have stuck with me throughout the years:

> Brothers and sisters: To the extent that God grants us to grow in Christian unity let us work together to offer strength and support to families, on whom the well-being of society depends and on whom our churches and ecclesial communities depend. May the families of America live with grateful hearts, giving thanks to the Lord for his blessings, praying for one another, bearing one another's burdens, welcoming one another as Christ has welcomed them. "May the grace of our Lord Jesus Christ be with you"
>
> (1 Thes 5:28)

Pope John Paul and Tony Melendez

Throughout the trip I witnessed hundreds of thousands of people who lined the streets of San Antonio, New Orleans, and Phoenix. However, I think that Pope John

Paul's visit to the Sheraton Universal Hotel in Los Angeles produced one of the most heartfelt scenes of his whole journey to America.

I arrived early for the pope's audience with leaders of the communications empire: heads of film studios, national television stations, film stars, CEOs of book publishing and similar media, and the like. I met "Moses": just a handshake with Charlton Heston who did not want any further visit. I drifted until facing Loretta Young, sitting royally in a chair and greeting people. She said to me, "Father, come and sit beside me," which I did for about fifteen minutes while she rolled on in her captivating theatrical style. It was a pleasure.

Across the front of the room were TV monitors showing the pope in a neighboring theater where he was reading his speech to a huge crowd of young people, his favorite kind of audience and one where he was always very effective. Everyone sat down but while he was reading, our audience paid little attention and spent the time chatting with each other. This changed when his talk was over and a young man spoke to the Holy Father with these words.

> Holy Father, the youth of our country offers you the following gifts of prayer.
>
> First, from St. Louis. "Holy Father we offer you the gift of prayer for the sanctity of human life from conception until natural death."

> From New York. "Holy Father. We give you the gift of concern for the poor, the forgotten, the unloved, all those who need out love, concern and help."

> From Chicago. "Holy Father, We offer you the gift of our commitment to purity of heart, mind and body."

As these scenes appeared on the screens our room became silent. The drama of young peoples' open confessions of values so central to human life touched us all.

Then came the scene never to be forgotten. The announcer said, "Holy Father, we now have a special gift for you. Our gift represents courage, a courage that comes from self-motivation and family support. Our gift is music and a performer who says, 'When I sing, I hear the Lord.' We are proud to present to you, Tony Melendez." The camera panned to an armless man sitting on a chair. He had a guitar beneath his bare feet, and he proceeded to play the instrument with his toes. He sang a song he had composed, "Never be the Same." Here are two verses.

> Today is filled with love
> Today is like no other day before
> You and I will never be the same.

> We become the sign of love
> Our God has given us
> We become the witness to his grace.

The young crowd stood and broke into long and loud applause. The camera was behind the pope when he stood with arms outstretched. He went down the steps and walked toward Tony. Then he appeared to fall, but actually he jumped down to the floor in front of Tony's platform. With his arms up he drew Tony to himself and hugged him. The camera showed Tony's face: a picture of awesome joy. The pope concluded with these words, "Tony, Tony, you are a courageous young man. You are an example of hope. My wish to you is to continue giving hope to all people."

The scene was so compelling that in our room three hundred tough, flinty titans of entertainment and business remained still and hushed for the next ten minutes. (If you would like to see this scene, Google "You Tube Pope John Paul and Tony Melendez.")

Then the pope came and spoke to the small group, still enthralled by what they had just witnessed. As one familiar with acting and writing poetry, Pope John Paul spoke with appreciation of the group's talents and gifts. He was aware of their influence on culture and society. He encouraged them to provide creative works that would build up virtues, behaviors, and attitudes that ennoble human dignity and promote a respect for life and a commitment to a morality that creates a society motivated to practice the highest ideals that all people of good will understand.

The audience applauded his address with enthusiasm. As we all were leaving the room, I heard many words of praise for his thoughts and, here and there, a sort of longing to implement his message.

Reflection

Throughout Pope John Paul's visit, he witnessed a new evangelization in the spirit of St. Paul and acted as a spiritual director to the nation in the spirit of St. John. How did he do it? He constantly preached the message, "Do not be afraid," an axiom he lived through his fearless life and teachings. He redefined the public ministry of the Bishop of Rome, roaming the world in over ninety trips as a living embodiment of the new evangelization. He showed us that we should not wait for people to come to Christ and the Church, rather, we need to bring Christ and the Church to the people. He broke the spell that had clouded the competing interpretations of Vatican II. He resolutely opposed those who saw the council as a revolutionary break with the past. Instead, he insisted on its continuity with the Church of the past.

In packed stadiums throughout the country, he led hundreds of thousands in celebrating the centerpiece of Catholicism, the Holy sacrifice of the Mass. His homilies centered on Jesus Christ, Lord and Savior of us all. He did more than talk about Jesus and his presence in the Holy Eucharist; he spoke as a man whose daily life is a conversation with Jesus. He did not just preach about a theological concept, he spoke as someone who trusted and confided in Jesus. His path of spiritual direction was a living echo of the Gospel of John, who devoted an entire chapter (chapter 6) to the truth of the Eucharist and chapters 15 through 17 to Christ's sermon on the impact of the Eucharist on our spiritual lives. At the end of those long, tiring days, he went before the Blessed Sacrament to be renewed and strengthened for the next day. Is it any wonder that the crowds at his funeral chanted, "*Santo Subito!*" ("Declare him a saint right now!")? Well, he is now Saint John Paul and his body rests in St. Peter's Basilica. He stressed that sanctity and holiness are relevant to the modern world. This is his legacy for us.

CHAPTER 18

Aid for a Persecuted Church

I was finishing my tasks regarding the papal visit when my Norbertine priest friend, Father Roman Vanasse, called me to discuss the need for a spiritual director for the American office of Church in Need. He had just completed his tenure at the Propagation of the Faith in New York City, and had then received an appointment as the Spiritual Director of Aid to the Church in Need in Koenigstein, Germany. Contributors to Aid to the Church in Need provided over 70 million dollars a year to sustain the persecuted Church behind the Iron Curtain, in Sudan, in China, and other hot spots of cruelty to those who held onto their faith in Christ and his Church.

The founder of this organization was a Norbertine member of an Abbey in Belgium. His name was Father Werenfried Van Straaten. After World War II, Western Europe was flooded with refugees from countries behind the Iron Curtain such as Poland, Czechoslovakia, Germany, and Hungary. Trouble arose when German refugees appeared on the scene, especially in Belgium which had suffered from German invasions during two world wars. Westerners were not inclined to help people from a country that had caused them so much pain and treated them cruelly. But Father Van Straaten persevered, preaching Christ's charity for the hungry, poor and homeless people who were former enemies.

He mounted pulpits all over Belgium and begged for money and food on their behalf. After Mass he stood at the church doors with his big hat held out for the offerings. Rejected at first, he stayed with the cause and prevailed. The farmers had little cash but they could offer bacon. This led to Werenfried being called the "bacon priest." As he became aware of the silent suffering of millions of Christians behind the iron curtain he founded Aid to the Church in Need. Eventually he established offices in thirteen countries to support the cause and extended the benefits to believers wherever they were persecuted.

Eventually I was appointed American spiritual director which involved preaching the cause, begging for funds in a number of parishes across the United States, as well as other duties. The main office was in Rockville Centre. The man in charge was Bob Lulley. He had the right personality for the task: cheerful, faith-filled, married to Ursula. Their faith was nourished by their membership in a spiritual society, Focolare, founded by a saintly Italian woman, Chiara Lubich. He helped me acquire a number of parishes to visit in the summer, preaching the cause and asking for donations. My main contact with him was by phone and letter, but we did meet in Germany for the annual gathering.

A Norbertine in Pilzen

Forbidden to be caring and charitable

Once a year, we all met at Koenigstein for a review of the various forms and intensity persecuted Catholics were facing around the world, the impact of our donors, support for them, and suggestions for improving all our offices. After our first meeting, Roman and I traveled to Czechoslovakia to visit Norbertine parishes and convents. Our first stop was at a parish in Pilzen. The pastor gave us a vivid picture of his life under Communist oppression. He was forbidden to dress as a priest. He was not allowed to hear confessions, bring Communion, or administer the sacrament of Anointing to the sick in the local nursing home.

He could celebrate Sunday Mass, but was forbidden to make any critical comments of the government in his sermons. A government agent attended all Masses, monitoring his words and behavior. The agent also had a list of the names of teenagers, and checked to see if any of them attended Mass. If they did they were warned to stop it, otherwise they would not be able to attend college. This practice caused young people to become indifferent to religion from their teen years through higher education. They went through their journey to adulthood without the support of faith, and, for the most part, learned to live without God. Many years later, the result is the triumph of secularization for most of them. It is why Pope Benedict called for a "new evangelization."

In recalling the pastor's plight, I am reminded about our own government attempting to separate freedom of worship from freedom of religion. We are free to worship in a church building, but freedom of religion, applying what our worship means in education, health care, marriage, justice for minorities and the working class is not to be allowed. Their first step is the "camel's nose" poking into the tent, forcing us to pay employees for birth control, sterilization, and morning-after abortifacient pills. Once the camel's nose is inside the tent of the Church's religious freedom, the whole camel will soon be inside. I saw it in Pilzen. On the happy side, the pastor said that the people were restless and had begun organizing a revolt. They now have freedom, but the harm has been done and so a "new evangelization" is necessary. They will have to re-learn how to rebuild a Christian culture.

Roman and I then went to Prague, where we visited our Norbertine Strahov Abbey. Over eight hundred years old, the Abbey buildings occupy a tract of land on what is called "Castle Hill." Other buildings nearby include palaces of former kings, St. Vitus Cathedral, and the archbishop's house where Cardinal Tomasek lived. At the foot of that hill, the Norbertines rented a building for their seminarians. That is where we stayed. The Soviet leadership did not allow new religious, so the novices were officially sponsored by the diocese, but were actually Norbertines. The government had preserved the Abbey building with its world famous libraries and treated it as a museum. The state had also spent millions to restore the church in exquisite detail. They allowed one Mass on Sunday to be celebrated by a Norbertine. We were able to see the Abbey and to enter the church which contains the body of St. Norbert. We were able to concelebrate Mass at the altar above which is enshrined Norbert's body.

We joined a group meeting with Cardinal Tomasek, famous for his opposition to the government. Several times he was asked, "Do you see the end of this oppressive government?" Silently, each time he raised his head and stared at the chandelier, reminding us that there was a microphone there monitored by government spies. At the same time, he communicated a hope that change for the better was underway. The Communist destruction of Christian culture was so absolute and its heavy hand still so present that it will take heroism of a major proportion to rebuild. It took centuries to create such a culture. And it will still require a lot of time to push back and rebuild. In spite of this, the inspiring people we met were determined to forge ahead.

After that, we had a meeting with some bishops in a private room. Twice, another bishop opened the door and scanned each of us with a hostile glance. We were told he was a "Pacem in Terris bishop," a government spy. These renegade prelates scandalously adopted the title of Pope John XXIII's glorious encyclical *Pacem in Terris* (Peace on Earth) to hide their militant intentions. It certainly was good to meet loyal bishops and priests; their courage was inspiring. But it was also clear they had a huge challenge to re-build the Church and a Christian culture, and had very few resources. Their confidence in Christ reminded me of the early apostles, heading into a dangerous world, with their profound trust in Christ's teachings and graces.

Mr. Cyril and Mr. Methodius . . . No!

One of the priests we met told us of the recent annual celebration of Saints Cyril and Methodius, the missionaries who brought Christianity to the Slavic peoples. They translated the Bible and the liturgy into the Slav language. They are models of how to adapt the faith to other cultures. They knew how to promote unity without rigid uniformity. They laid the foundation of a truly Christian popular culture. This particular year, thousands of young people filled the plaza for the celebration.

The government sent their pagan officers to lead the service. As was their custom they praised Mr. Cyril and Mr. Methodius. To which the thousands of young voices responded, "No! No! Saint Cyril! Saint Methodius!" And "Long Live the Pope!" They drowned out the pagans. They kept chanting and singing their own prayer service until the agent left the platform. A fresh breeze was in the air. Even ancient saints were acclaimed. Yes, it will take time. But, I believe the Holy Spirit is there to stay.

A Concentration Convent

Roman and I were exhilarated by our visits to Pilzen and Prague. Things got even better when we visited the Norbertine Sisters of Radvanov in Slovakia. When the Communists took over, they decreed that the nuns, who worked in schools, hospitals, orphanages, and shelters for the homeless, would no longer be allowed to engage in public acts of charity. The world was not to know Catholicism's face of kindness, care and love. Only the State would be allowed to do that with cold eyes and careless hands.

Our Norbertine sisters were told that if they wanted to remain nuns, they would have to live unseen and unheard in the Motherhouse, now redubbed a Concentration Convent. For forty years, the Norbertine Sisters of Radvanov Convent lived behind their walls. They lived as cloistered nuns with a full schedule of prayer and care for each other and continued to learn how to grow as a community in these circumstances. No new vocations were allowed until the State allowed young women to join so they could care for the elderly sisters and save the government that responsibility. As a result, there were a great number of new vocations, so the government imposed a limit on new candidates.

At Radvanov Convent, we discovered a community of Sisters that were cheerful, lively, enthusiastic, and highly motivated. They looked forward to the end of this system and were ready to go forth and serve. I can still hear their laughter. I was reminded of one of my favorite childhood movies, *The Bells of St. Mary's* with its teaching nuns in the slums, laughing, crying, and shamelessly joyful. The Radvanov nuns were realistic, tough, and caring. They harbored no illusions about the government, but remained rock hard in their faith in Christ, whom they served behind walls for forty years.

Mother Russia

The following year, I visited the few sites we were able to support in Russia in those days. The first stop was at St. Louis Church, the only active Catholic Church in Moscow at that time. The Assumptionist Fathers have been in charge of the church since 1932, when President Roosevelt made a treaty with Stalin to allow one church in the city to be available for embassy staff. I was fortunate enough to meet Father Josef Guncaga who showed me around and expressed appreciation for the support received from our organization. I noted that the church was located on Lubyanka Street, one block from the KGB Lubyanka prison, the fearful center of Stalin's purges. It was also where Jesuit Father Walter Ciczek was imprisoned for a time before being sent to a gulag. Among memories of courage in enduring endless suffering, he is the author of this insight into faith: "Faith is like a dark tunnel. God gives you the light to take one step at a time. The light is not given to see the end of the tunnel."

When I left the church, I saw the prison down the

block. As I took a picture of it, I had the nervous feeling someone there was taking a picture of me.

That afternoon I visited the apartment of Assumptionist Father Norman Micklejohn. He served as chaplain to the American Embassy where he celebrated Mass for Catholics from all the embassies. Across the hall from his apartment, he created the chapel of Our Lady of Good Hope where he offered daily Mass. At dinner I met another Assumptionist Father, Bernard Le Leannec. He was also on the staff of St. Louis church, and ministered to Mother Teresa's nuns in the city. He told me a fascinating story.

To get a better understanding of the Orthodox Church, he spent a year at the Zagorsk monastery, one of the few Stalin allowed to survive. (You can see it on You Tube "Zagorsk,"—the film accompanied by a heart-swelling Russian choir.) He said they had three hundred monks and seven hundred seminarians, mostly married. He had, obviously, loved his year there and spoke movingly about their devotion to the mysticism of St. John's Gospel, their formation through the liturgy and the Jesus or Heart prayer said with beads held on one's left hand— closest to one's heart.

I then took a plane to St. Petersburg. My seat-mate spoke good English and told me he was a trained physicist, married with children and living in an apartment like most Russians. I recall his telling me about his salary. It was quite small considering his training as a scientist and his value to the state. He mentioned the time it took to save up enough to get a car, a TV set, or other items we take for granted.

St. Petersburg, then renamed Leningrad, once so grand, looked shabby. The main avenue, called the Nevsky Prospect, is three miles long. At one end is the world famous art museum, the Hermitage. At other end is the Nevsky Monastery. In between are stores of all kinds that had little to display. The grandeur of royal days had long gone. I stayed at a hotel across from the Nevsky monastery, which was filled every day with pilgrims. I went there each day for their morning prayer. A cantor sang psalms, scripture readings, and responses. I was struck by the way the people, walking around, praying before their favorite icons, would break into four-part harmony and sing the responsorial psalm to the readings. Given our knowledge of the volcanic efforts of the state to crush Christianity, it was amazing to me how parts of the Church still endure, no matter what.

My second day, I went to visit the only Catholic Church in St. Petersburg, Our Lady of Lourdes. It was around mid-morning when I arrived. The Church was well cared for and modestly decorated. I was alone. Then I heard noise coming from the sacristy. I went there and met the pastor, Father Josef Provilonis. It was a bit awkward. I could not speak Russian. He could not speak English. Gradually, I recalled my Latin and identified myself and Aid to the Church in Need. He warmed up right away and asked, "*Pater, velisne Missam celebrare?*"

I answered "*Utique, Pater.*" He showed me the vestments and lit the candles.

He found a Latin Missal and I was ready for Mass. A group of college students drifted in and attended. As this former ten-year inmate of a gulag stood by my side, I read the first sentence from Acts 8:1: "*In illo tempore* . . . On that day a persecution broke out in the Church." Reading those words, standing next to a veteran of suffering for Christ, I fully realized I was in the land of martyrs, where 50,000 priests were liquidated and 40,000 churches were closed in seventy years. After Mass I teased him about bringing him some rubles, which, due to inflation, were not worth much. Before he got too disappointed, I gave him a substantial gift of American dollars. We parted with mutual blessings. A number of young people had waited for me outside and wanted to talk about America. They had been listening on their radios to sermons from mega-church preachers. I urged them to tune into Mother Angelica's EWTN Radio which was now beamed to Russia.

This visit more than any confirmed my admiration for Aid to the Church in Need and the generous donors that helped increase the hope and faith of many thousands of people.

CHAPTER 19

The New Catechism

> I rarely preach a sermon, but I go to this beautiful and complete catechism, to get both my matter and my doctrine.
>
> —Cardinal John Henry Newman

IN the above quote, Cardinal Newman was referring to the *Roman Catechism*, commissioned by the Council of Trent in 1546 and published in 1566. I enjoy reminding myself and those I know about this fascinating confession by one of the greatest preachers and theologians in our history. As an Anglican, he was already one of the most popular and revered preachers at Oxford. As a Catholic convert, his preaching skills continued in his homilies. I admire his humility in his reference to the *Roman Catechism*. The term catechism for those of us from an older generation raises pictures of small booklets with questions and brief responses which were often easy to memorize. The *Roman Catechism* was a thick book covering the Creed, Morality, Worship, and Prayer. Church historians will note that such a document may be credited for being the standard of faith for Catholics. It was a sure guide for their beliefs, attitudes, and behavior.

For four centuries it was a rock on which believers could stand in perilous times, especially during the hurricane unleashed by the Reformation.

On June 25, 1992, I read that Pope John Paul II had announced the publication of the new *Catechism of the Catholic Church*. A few months later I was visiting a priest friend, Monsignor Michael Wrenn, pastor of St. John's Church in Manhattan. I saw on his coffee table a copy of the new catechism. I was surprised that it was written in French instead of Latin as I would have expected. Fortunately, because of my year of training in French at Lumen Vitae, I was able to understand the text. Msgr. Wrenn had several copies and let me take one.

If anyone doubts the need for such a catechism, there is a sobering message from studies that claim religious illiteracy is widespread. Gallup Poll surveys show that two thirds of Catholics do not know the correct meaning of the Eucharist, or that Jesus delivered the Sermon on the Mount and composed the Our Father. The new *Catechism* was a providential response to the awakened religious spirit of many Catholics who see the need for religious literacy for themselves and their children.

It occurred to me that many people would appreciate an introduction to this new catechism. I proposed the possibility of doing an introduction to the new catechism to Robert Lockwood, publisher of Our Sunday Visitor Press. Eventually, this came about and I wrote, *Essentials of the Faith: A Guide to the Catechism of the Catholic Church*. I knew there would be a need to help parishes and schools make this catechism accessible to students, volunteer teachers, preachers who sought ways to use it for sermons and those involved with helping converts appreciate our teachings. It became a long-time bestseller.

A Teen Catechism

When he saw my book, Father Bradley encouraged me to write a similar book for teens. Bob Gallagher, the president of Good Will Publishers seconded Bradley's request and I accepted the idea.

In my seminary years before the Second Vatican Council, the writings of St. Thomas Aquinas influenced our professors who taught us his philosophy and his approach to theology. It occurred to me that it might be a good idea to borrow from and adapt the way St. Thomas provided an outline for each teaching. He began with a question, followed by a series of answers that were wrong or incomplete. Then he would note his own reply, followed by reasons why the false answers were incorrect or inadequate. When I taught teens, I often noticed they liked raising questions. In their growth period, they were discovering new horizons in their lives.

With that in mind, I developed a catechism in which each new topic began with a question. For example, "Is the Bible alone the sole source of God's revelation?" Before replying directly to the question, I started with a faith story, often the life of a saint or famous Catholic. I often used inspiring conversion stories, which appealed to the imagination of the student and involved him more deeply in the questions. Biographies, autobiographies and self-sacrifice narratives have a heroic quality that attracts young minds and hearts.

I followed the question and faith story with three replies.

(1)   **Several wrong or inadequate answers.**
        This method allows the text to introduce misunderstandings of Catholic teachings in a context of dialogue where shedding light on the truth can become more evident

(2)   **A response from the catechism; the Church's teaching.** I did this by creating three questions with answers from the Catechism. It offered the student a sure norm of Catholic teaching and helped the student get into the Catechism and explore it further.

(3)   **Reasons why the first reply was wrong or inadequate.** The third response to the question follows up on the first one, correcting other misunderstandings and offering more thoughts on the question.

I concluded each lesson with an "In My Life" section, applying the teaching to the students, a prayer, and, finally, a glossary of terms.

By the end of the text, the students would have a faith vocabulary to express their beliefs. The book was published by Our Sunday Visitor and widely used.

Bishop Baker, then of the Charleston Diocese of South Carolina, gave copies of the book to newly confirmed young people. Bob Gallagher adopted the book by getting sponsors to pay for a number of copies that would be given free to students. This approach provided a huge number of young people with complimentary copies and the wisdom of the catechism for their Catholic faith life. May God bless Bob Gallagher for this contribution to the growth in faith of our young people. In the meantime, I became a member of the Good Will Group board and have served there for more than twenty years.

CHAPTER 20

Appointment to Blessed John Seminary

A LL of us have a mysterious call from God for our lives. Some pay attention to it and some do not. With that in mind, before sharing the next stage in my life, allow me to meditate on Mother Teresa's explanation of her call to help the poor. David Porter tells that story this way:

> "This is how it happened," she told me. "I was traveling to Darjeeling by train when I heard the voice of God" When I asked her how she heard this voice above the noise of a rattling train, she replied with a smile. "I was sure it was God's voice. I was certain he was calling me. The message was clear: I must leave the convent to help the poor by living among them. This was a command, something to be done, something definite. I knew where I had to be. I did not know how to get there."
>
> As she spoke, her face glowed with happiness, peace and assurance. I wondered—was a vision or an inspiration? Did she hear a voice— or something else? In view of what else was

going on, how could she be sure?

She broke into my thoughts. "The form of the call is neither here nor there. It was something between God and me. What matters is that God calls each of us in a different way. It is not credit to us that he does so. What matters is that we should answer the call! In those difficult and dramatic days I was certain this was God's doing and not mine, and I am still certain, And, as it was the work of God I knew the world would benefit from it."

(*Mother Teresa, the Early Years* by David Portman,
Eerdmans. Grand Rapids, 1986, page 56)

In my life, God usually has reached me through other people, some being friends and others interested strangers. In 1994, my former student, Father Jim Hawker, director of religious education for the archdiocese of Boston, called me to say that Cardinal Law would like me to come to Boston to introduce the new Catechism to all groups involved in catechesis. I would be meeting with teachers in the schools and parishes, pastors, chaplains at universities and colleges. At first it was thought I would stay at a parish, but eventually the possibility of residing at Pope John XXIII Seminary in Weston, Massachusetts, emerged.

Cardinal Cushing believed that God called some older men to priestly vocations and created this seminary to serve them. At the time he thought of this, the local St.

John Seminary was filled with students, so the Cardinal was not thinking of the shortage of vocations. But his concept has flourished and has provided a steady flow of priests to serve the Church in many dioceses.

In a conversation I had with the Rector, Monsignor Cornelius (Connie) McCrae, who favored the idea and warmly welcomed me to live at the seminary, he asked me to offer a course on the Catechism as an elective for the students. The student body was composed of older men, a mix of widowers and unmarried men, most of whom were in their forties. People spoke of them as second-career men. Monsignor Francis Kelly, whom I have mentioned many times in this book, was on the faculty and helped me to adapt to this new setting.

Over the course of that academic year, I developed core lectures on the Catechism. The novelty of such a catechism made it easier to explain because the curiosity about it was a natural response. Virtually everyone was pleased at the primacy of scripture and liturgy in the text. Every chapter opened with the scriptural source of the teaching and frequently cited liturgical texts and ceremonies that illustrated the doctrine. The great advantage of this fact supported the "relationship with God, Father, Son and Spirit" as an essential aspect of the teaching.

On every page is the living God, revealing himself and inviting us to faith and love. The Catechism was never meant to be a dry text or collection of intellectualized truths. Its goal is union with God's active and salvific presence. The fruits of this catechism are a dynamic, lifelong relationship of Christ with each of us in the communion of the Church by the power of the Spirit. This is why I always framed catechetical teachings with lives of the saints and other heroic Catholics and closed with living applications of the message. There is a human and humanitarian side to all doctrines because of Christ's incarnational reality. St. Paul dramatizes this fact over and over, best seen when he writes,

> Have among yourselves the same attitude that also yours in Christ Jesus, who, though he was in the form of God, did not regard equality with God something to be grasped. Rather, he emptied himself, taking the form of a slave, coming in human likeness, and found human in appearance.
>
> (Phil 2:5–7)

Readers and students also liked the Catechism's relationship to Church history, which expressed the development of doctrine through the ages in the manner Cardinal Newman had explained in his masterpiece on this aspect of Church teaching. This was done effectively with quotes from lives of saints and excellent citations from Saints Augustine, Chrysosotom, Aquinas, and many others. Veteran teachers, especially, could see the Catechism's clear organization of the material based on a model that appeared in every chapter.

In a similar spirit, I often mentioned that the fourth part of the text, which was devoted to prayer, should be applied throughout the whole book. It is not enough to talk about God. It is essential that we converse with Him. Recall how often the Bible exhorts us to "Hear the Word of the Lord."

What? Original Sin!

During the year I was meeting with different audiences for the archdiocese, I found the teachers and pastors willing to learn about the Catechism and interested in applying its contents to their various ministries. There were no incidents and very little in the way of arguments even with the chaplains to the colleges and universities.

However, toward the end of the year, I had an experience that stays in my memory to this day. It occurred in a large auditorium. All the seats were filled with about eight hundred teachers. The audience represented the Catholic elementary schools and parish programs of that section of the archdiocese. The listeners were attentive and seemed content with my presentation, when I happened to say, mostly as a tease, "Well, I am finished. I assume you all agreed with me?" I don't know why I said that, since it was not normal with me.

All did not agree. From the right side of the auditorium in the back corner, a roar came up with a definite "NO!" Shocked, I fumbled back, "What do you mean, 'No?'" One of the teachers stood and said, "You obviously have no experience with children. In your discussion of original sin you attributed its effect on our evil behavior.

Even on children." I replied, "Please be seated and allow me to do my duty as a teacher of Catholic doctrine." And I briefly reviewed again what the Bible and the Church mean by original sin. I also invited the audience in general to give their thoughts, which they did. All the immediate respondents, mostly laity, supported my positions on the topic, commenting on the parental experiences of very young children quarreling, being envious, fighting, needing to be trained in obedience and being considerate of others, and requiring discipline.

I explained that in speaking of original sin, we do not attribute moral evil to younger children in the same sense we speak of it in older children, teens, and adults. Rather, we note the need for training the very young on issues of good and bad behavior, and, at some point, its scriptural foundation of the doctrine of original sin. I then invited the teacher to have the last word. She said, "I guess I don't belong here." Afterwards I met with the regional superintendent and urged her to have someone with pastoral skills meet with her and urge her to reconsider her views as well as with the several rows of teachers who had joined in the chorus of dissent.

Here and there, I had become aware of dislike for the doctrine of original sin, some dismissing it as a later doctrine cooked up by St. Augustine, others claiming that the Eastern Churches did not agree with it. I would reply that St. Augustine coined the term but did not invent the teaching, which he eloquently explained was consistent with the apostolic Fathers and the Churches of the East.

The real problem, I believed, was the denial of the reality of sin in general and the need for Christ's redemption. I think the decline of Confession is a proof of this. Bishop Sheen sensed it years earlier when he quipped, "Everyone thinks they are immaculately conceived."

Training Second Career Seminarians

As my year introducing the Catechism to the archdiocese came to an end, I heard that the faculty at Blessed John XXIII Seminary were about the vote on whether I would be invited to become a member of the faculty. In June 1994, they voted yes and I was made a full-time professor. My main task was to teach the homiletic courses to freshmen and juniors. I also continued my course on Catechetics. Over time, I also developed optional courses entitled, "Images of Mary," "The Book of Revelation," and "Apologetics."

Training Preachers

I especially loved teaching preaching since it meant being personally involved with the students at every minute of each class, instead of lecturing and wondering what goes on in their minds, as was customary in the other classes, despite all efforts at discussion and other forms of student/professor involvement. I had them for a class in preaching in the first year and met them again for a class in their third year. After an orientation in the opening class, I had one student give a sermon or homily each week during the semester. The third year went smoother than the first because they had more experience as well as a deeper well of theology, liturgy, and scripture training to draw from.

My rules were the same for both the first and third years. Everyone must preach a five- to seven-minute homily every week. I expected them to begin with a story that illustrated the message from scripture. I explained that relevant stories captured the imagination of the listeners. This rescued the congregation from various distractions.

They were not allowed to read a text or notes, unless they suffered from attention deficit disorder, or were afflicted with dyslexia, or some other stumbling block, such as stuttering. If they were immigrants, I would also permit using notes, though I pushed them to take summer courses in accent reduction, reminding them that their congregations needed to understand what they were saying. I required them to have only one clear point for their talk. By not using notes or a written text, they would be able to look at the people they were addressing, which would not only help them connect to the audience, but would also help them discern whether they appeared interested, fascinated, unhappy, or indifferent. I reminded them that preaching is an event that united speaker and audience in a mysterious human interaction.

I suggested they memorize their last sentence so they would know where to land. I encouraged them to search the congregation for faces that look pleased with their efforts. This can build confidence. While they would mostly be bound to a lectern or pulpit, I did not allow any such prop in the classroom. I wanted them to feel as close to the listeners as possible. I gave them hints on effective ways to outline their talks and avoid memorizing the text. I approved their memorizing the bare outlines of their homilies.

I emphasized the need to be prayerful, faith-filled and saturated in scripture as much as they could. Today, I would speak somewhat like evangelicals do in such matters. Vivid familiarity with the Gospels and Epistles as well as writings of the titans of spirituality is essential for preaching. However, holding the Bible in one hand needs to be balanced with the newspaper, or computer, or iPod, or whatever is necessary. Jesus talked mainly to farmers and shepherds and grape growers. That is why crops and lambs and wine accompany his homilies. Today he would probably use Twitter as an example. Preaching Christ is the top requirement. Soak your life in the Gospels and St. Paul.

Home to Rome

In 2000, we received the joyful news that Pope John XXIII, our seminary's namesake, was going to be beatified, so plans were made for attending the ceremony in Rome. On the day of the event, we were standing in front of St. Peter's basilica in the middle of a huge crowd. I learned that my spiritual friend, Abbot Columba Marmion was also being beatified. Gratefully I looked back to my seminary days when I would read and re-read Christ the Ideal of the Monk and Christ, the Life of the Soul. His words come back to me now:

> Never tire of hearing Jesus spoken of. Never weary of it. Even to think of Jesus, to look at him with faith, brings us holiness. Christ is not only a model such as an artist looks at when he paints a picture. Christ is more than a model. God is not content with a natural religion or morality. God wills us to act as children of a divine race. Each of our Lord's actions is not only a model for us, but also a source of grace. In practicing all the virtues, Jesus merited for us the grace to be able to practice all the virtues which we contemplate in him.
>
> (Adapted from *Christ the Life of the Soul*, Herder. St. Louis, pp. 60–61)

On our final night in Rome, Msgr. Kelly arranged a farewell supper at an outdoor restaurant in a park-like setting. The guest of honor was Cardinal Francis Xavier Van Tuan. After supper he gave a brief speech about his sufferings in Vietnam. The same week that the American military left Saigon, Van Tuan, then a bishop, was imprisoned for his refusal to bow to the tyranny of the Communist regime.

For the next thirteen years, he was condemned to

solitary confinement. In time he gained the confidence of his guards. He asked them for a bar of soap, a piece of wood, some wire, and a knife. With the knife, he carved a cross with the wood and cut the soap in half where he hid the cross. Later, he persuaded the guard to bring him a tiny cup of wine and some bread. With these elements he offered Mass in his cell. He wore no liturgical garb, possessed no missal, nor lectionary, but recited what he could remember. While there were no other worshipers present, he knew that angels from heaven filled his cell and adored the Eucharistic Lord who was made present through his celebration.

We were all enchanted by his presence and his heroic story of faith under fire. Asked what his role was now, the Cardinal replied, "I work for the office of Justice and Peace." Asked, "What does this entail?" He replied, "I am sent to mediate people who have failed to communicate with each other. I am good at living and working with those who did not love me. That is the gift God has awarded me." Then the pilgrimage was over and we were back in the seminary and our respective classes within the week.

The Real Agenda of Vatican II

Off and on, I was invited to do a thirteen part series for EWTN. In 1996, one of these experiences was about the life and teachings of Pope John XXIII. Whenever I did a series, I would also be a guest on Mother Angelica Live on

Wednesday nights. That year, she wore a black patch over one eye, due to a stroke. Normally, before a show, Mother would be given a dose of oxygen in the corridor to help her keep up her voice for the TV hour. But something was different this time. When she began to introduce me, her voice was barely audible. She mentioned that some people were not comfortable with Pope John, "but Father McBride will help you to appreciate him."

I waited a moment for her to continue, since that's what usually occurred. She would take ten minutes or more to chat with the TV audience and the guests in the room. Then she would have the guest begin the conversation in which she would participate. But, this time she whispered, "Go ahead, Father." I had brought with me five points of a vision for the Council that Pope John made in his talk opening the Council.

I began with his first point: "Don't be a prophet of gloom. Prophets of gloom have a pessimistic view of the world and the Church. They should not set the tone for the Council. We feel we much disagree with them . . . Providence is leading us to a new order of human relations that is directed to fulfilling God's saving plan."

I waited. Mother nodded. **I went on to his second point: "Teach the faith more effectively.** The greatest concern of an Ecumenical Council is this: that the sacred deposit of Christian doctrine should be guarded and taught more effectively. The Church should never depart from the sacred patrimony of Truth received from the Fathers." There would be no hermeneutics of discontinuity.

I waited again. She nodded and gestured to keep going, which I did for the rest of my part of the program. **I went on to point three:** "The principal purpose of this Council is not a discussion of the Church's doctrines. No Council was necessary for this. **What is expected is "a step forward in understanding of the doctrine and assistance in forming people's consciences.** *Fides quarens intellectum.*

   a. Doctrine should be studied and explained through methods of research and literary forms of modern thought.
   b. The substance of an ancient doctrine is one thing. The way it is presented is another such as Church as organization or as *Communio*.

I went on with point four: What about modern errors?

   a. The Church always opposes errors. Sometimes she condemns them.
   b. Today, the spouse of Christ prefers the medicine of mercy rather than severity.
   c. Demonstrate the validity of the Church's teachings rather than condemnation.

I **finished with point five: Promote the unity of all peoples.**

   a. Unity within the Church.
   b. Unity with Christians separated from Catholicism
   c. Unity with those who follow non-Christian religions.

A few months later Mother Angelica had her second stroke and retired. May God bless her for her extraordinary contributions to the Church.

Golden Jubilee

In the final months of my last year at the seminary, I was privileged to celebrate the fiftieth anniversary of my priesthood. Since it was also the golden jubilee of priesthood of my friend Father Charles Healy, S.J., the two of us celebrated together. He was the principal celebrant of the Mass and I preached the homily. The chapel was full and so were the dinner tables after Mass. I was thrilled to be able to celebrate this anniversary with fellow priests, including Father James Hawker who sat in the front pew, and those who were planning to become priests. I am grateful to Msgr. Kelly for overseeing the celebration with his eye for detail and his loving heart for the priesthood. I also thank Father John O'Brien pastor of Sacred Heart in Quincy, where I served as a Sunday Mass celebrant for ten years, for providing a parish reception for me after Mass.

I also wanted to have a Mass of Thanksgiving at St. Patrick's in Philadelphia. Since I would have a small crowd I thought it would be better to have the Mass in the Lower Church which would be, so I thought, a more friendly atmosphere. The pastor, Monsignor Philip Dowling, judged otherwise. He said, "Al come with me for a tour of the Upper Church before you make your decision." He had all the lights on as we walked from the front door into the church building I loved so well and in which I had spent so many years. It was exactly as I remembered it and was gleaming from floor to ceiling. By the time I reached the steps leading to the altar, I was convinced that I would have the privilege of offering the Eucharist in this place where I had my first Mass.

Bob Moccia and his wife Ria chose for the reception a dining room at the new Rittenhouse Hotel, built on the land where the Notre Dame de Namur Nuns had once conducted an academy for youth. I invited as many of my childhood friends as I could recall as well as Norbertine members of Daylesford Abbey and two archdiocesan priests, Msgr. Michael Carroll, a close friend who was a leader of religious education in Philadelphia, and Father John Dougherty, raised on Pine Street a few doors down from my home.

It was a lovely occasion. In procession down the aisle, I was delighted to see Jim and Dorothy Youniss who drove in from Washington and from whom I often received hospitality. Family members came in from California: Ed, Anne, and Lared Dougherty as well as Larry, Therese, and Ciaran Dougherty. Finbar and Mary McEvoy came from Berwyn.

The dinner went well. Childhood friends were there, including Joe Gorman and his sister Mary, Mike McHugh and his brother, Jack Robinson, Bob and Ria Moccia, and Tom Gavin's sister. Among the Norbertines were Abbot Neitzel, Abbot Thomas Rossi, his brother, Father Ron

Rossi, and Father Joseph Serano. I would also like to think that invisible guests were also at that table: Mary Courtney, her brother and sisters, Michael Corcoran, Sarah and Elizabeth Corcoran, Frank and Catherine Dougherty. They helped raise me just when I needed it. May God be good to them.

The music from the parish choir set the tone. The Norbertines, in their white habits were sitting in sanctuary choir stalls. I was surprised to see a contingent of college-age students who came over from the campus of the University of Pennsylvania. The Mass was beautiful and I was overwhelmed with memories and feelings.

A Small Reflection About Big Friends and Love

One of the reasons I was privileged to gather some good friends around me for a celebration is that I was attracted to the teaching of Jesus that I should not just love him, but accept the love he offers me. I have seen many people rush toward love with open arms, but then hide from it when love is offered to them. Why does this happen? Perhaps because they have been betrayed too often. The love offered to them was insincere. People fail to accept another's love because too many have let them down. Such people are paralyzed by fear. In that sense fear is the opposite of love. Many people are scared to accept love because they feel unable to return it.

They have not understood that another's love for them creates in them the capacity respond with love.

They have never accepted St. Paul's wise advice to the Romans that they should let the Holy Spirit of God's love into their lives so they can rise from the death of unlove. The people who gathered round me at my jubilee came with the affection of years, affection that distance did not dim. They knew I accepted their love and returned it. That is the beauty of the Christian contract. Such love is free and never taxed.

CHAPTER 21

Thanks to Jesus and Mary

O Jesus, when I have food,
help me to remember the hungry;
When I have work,
help me to remember the jobless;
When I have a home,
help me to remember those
who have no home at all;
When I am without pain,
help me to remember those who suffer

And remembering me, Blessed Mary,
help me to destroy my complacency;
bestir my compassion,
and be concerned enough to help;
by word and deed,
those who cry out
for what we take for granted. Amen

—Traditional Thanksgiving Prayer Slightly Adapted

Last But By No Means Least

In autumn, 2003, I was welcomed by Father Brian Prunty, the house superior, and the other Norbertine members of St. Joseph Priory as a member of their community. Situated on the bank of the Fox River and the campus of St. Norbert College, the community is an ideal way to live out what has been officially my retirement years. I have not been vegetating. God has blessed me with good health that allows me to walk three miles a day on this lovely campus and the neighboring tree-lined streets. I have continued writing and have published six new books in the last ten years.

I became involved in a small way in the founding of a new Catholic radio station, Relevant Radio, where I usually broadcast Mass on Wednesdays. I continue to serve on the Boards of *Our Sunday Visitor* and the Good Will Group of Charlotte, NC. I also serve as a trustee of the Norbertine Augustine Stewardship Fund and help out for parish Masses when I am free. I have discovered the pleasures of gardening despite the brief summer of northeast Wisconsin. Occasionally I am called to offer a Mass and a brief talk for a Catholic Men's group, "*Esto Vir*" (Be a Man).

Bishop Ricken has engaged me to write a catechesis for all the staff members of the diocese of Green Bay. They meet once a month during the school year and discuss my chapters in small groups with a leader selected by the bishop. As of this writing, they are completing the third year of study on the Church's teaching on morality. From time to time, I am invited to give clergy conferences around the country.

It helps immensely to be a member of a Norbertine community whose friendship and personal support supply me with the energy to go on. Let me introduce you to them, all priests. One is Peter Renard, who was a novice of mine years ago. He likes to remind me of those days, especially the funny ones, which I love to hear. Another former novice of mine is Father John Bostwick who is a professor of theology at our college. He is a thoughtful man who likes detective stories such as those of P. D. James and is generous enough to share them with me. I always enjoy listening to his homilies at our community Mass. He has the gift of wisdom and simplicity. Father Brian Prunty is a credentialed Physician's Assistant and can be counted on to impart all kinds of medical insights and information which we constantly bring to him. He often recalls his days in this capacity at the Cook County Jail in Chicago. He also has an active sense of humor that keeps us going.

Father Tim Shillcox is pastor of Our Lady of Lourdes parish here in West De Pere. He pastors a large, beautiful church that seats over a thousand people. He is blessed with pastoral gifts that endear him to his large congregation. He does not let the busy work of a parish prevent him from being present with us and part of our communal life. One thing I notice is his remarkable memory especially of people's ages and various ministries. He is tireless in helping out here as well as at the parish.

Father Conrad Kratz, another of my former novices, is a gifted priest with a huge following in the Green Bay–De Pere area and a successful head of our spiritual life center. Sadly, he suffered a severe stroke in 2011. It took him nearly a year to conquer the drawbacks of speech and movement. But he had been edging back on both accounts, when his health turned for the worse and he eventually died. A huge, saddened crowd joined us in mourning his passage and his legacy of joy.

Ninety-year-old Father Brendan McKeough is our senior member, a dutiful patron of the daily crossword puzzle, a Green Bay Packer fan, and an ardent supporter of the Church's social doctrine. He lived and served among the poorest of the poor in Mexico for over fifteen years. He has a great sense of humor and is a lively conversationalist. He helps out with the Hispanic Sunday Masses at our Norbertine parish, St. Willibrord's in Green Bay. He was an active soldier in World War II and served in the South Pacific. That is why he was a late vocation. We were ordained together. He was kind enough to me to have me join him, his parents, and his aunt, Bernice, for a wonderful vacation to Yosemite National Park and his parents gave me a Christmas present of Aquinas' Summa.

Father Gery Meehan has been a friend of mine since our earliest days in the Order. He was also born and raised in Philadelphia and for a time he and his family lived in West Philly not far from where my relatives lived. He asked me to preach his First Mass at the grand

Transfiguration church. We each preached at each other's Silver jubilees. He has a natural sense of humor, especially in the puns department. He survived a series of operations a few years ago and is active in local parishes. As pastor of our College church, he oversaw a stunning renovation that added a gathering space as well as a choir chapel that we use for Morning and Evening Prayer.

Father Rowland de Peaux at eighty-six is a lively member of the St. Norbert College Alumni association. He is present at most of their gatherings and travels to various city meetings with Todd Danen who supervises the association. But his greatest love is singing in the Dudley Birder Chorale, which has over one hundred singers and presents several marvelous concerts each year that draw packed theaters. The most famous of these musical events is the All Saints concert that pays tribute to one of our most revered Norbertines, Father Joseph Dorff.

Until this year Father Jim Baraniak was an active member of the priory community. He has just resigned after many years as pastor of Old St. Joseph's, the college church, and moved to the Abbey. He continues to be chaplain to the Green Bay Packers and offers Mass on Thursday mornings for the prisoners at the Wisconsin facility for young prisoners. He is also on the board of Catholic Athletes for Christ.

We have recently welcomed three new members to our community. Father Jay Fostner is Vice President for Mission and Heritage office at the college and also serves as director of Student Life there. He is cheerful, busy, and becoming increasingly active in our community life. The same is true of Father Dane Radecki who recently retired from being pastor of St. Agnes parish in Green Bay in order to accept Bishop Ricken's appointment as president of the Grace program. He is no stranger to the priory since he lived here during his tenure as founder of the Mission and Heritage office. He moved in with us to make it easier for him to oversee the General Chapter of the Norbertine Order on our campus, a task in which he excelled.

Our third new member is Father Andrew Ciferni, a priest from Daylesford Abbey in the suburbs of Philadelphia. He is an expert on liturgy and the history of our Order. Our college has appointed him Director of the Center for Norbertine Studies.

Last Words: The Joy of Real Community

In reviewing my fellow Norbertines, I kept noting their humor. I am reminded of Jesuit James Martin's book, *Between Heaven and Mirth*. He knows the value of a good laugh. Our community at St. Joe Priory has that wholesome glue in abundance that binds our hearts together. I would like to think we have a divine sense of humor. In order to laugh at a joke, we have to see the point. We say that people have no sense of humor because they don't see the point. God has made the world in such a way that he is the point of all we see. The world around us is a window through which we may see God. Mountains tell us of his power and snowflakes sing of his purity. The poor, hungry, and naked are Jesus in disguise. The point of creation is the Creator.

All sins are missing the point. The Hebrew word for sin means missing the mark. Sinners grab things as ends in themselves instead of roads to God. Sinners are too solemn about this world. It is too important to them. So they miss the point and therefore miss the God who would make them happy. In order to be joyful, you should not always be looking for a good time. There will be no fun in life if everything is supposed to be funny. At its base the source of joy is a quest for the infinite. Every joy attracts us because we sense there will be yet a more boundless joy. No one thing or person seems to satisfy us because we notice that we have an appetite for every-thing. The joy of a great party at night often yields to next day's hangover.

Joy is more than jokes. If there is joy in our commu-nity, it is due to the active presence of God in the hearts of our men. God our Father is infinitely joyful. If we make friends with God, we will share his joy. The spir-ituality of a Norbertine is based on a lifelong growth in intimacy with God through his Son Jesus under the guid-ance of the Holy Spirit. In community life, this contact with divine joy makes dealing with the challenges from each member's personality differences easier to face. We are all in a growth pattern from the moment we entered until the day of our deaths.

God's gift of his joy is the secret of becoming a true

Norbertine community. It is what St. Paul meant when he wrote,

> Complete my joy by being of the same mind, with the same love, united in heart, thinking one thing: Do nothing out of selfishness or out of vainglory. Rather humbly regard others as more important than yourselves.
>
> (Phil 2:2–3)

We have learned this the hard way by overcoming our sins and faults and staying as close to Christ as possible. St. James tells us that joy is connected with difficulties:

> Consider it all joy my brothers when you encounter various trials, for you know the testing of your faith produces perseverance. But if any one you lacks wisdom, he should ask God who gives to all generously and ungrudgingly, and he will be given it.
>
> (Jas 1:2–3; 5–6.)

Advisers for increasing membership in our community often stress the need for our members to live such a way that they attract those who are searching for a way to fulfill their vocation. I know what they mean. It was exactly that which drew me to the Norbertines after four years in their high school in Philadelphia. All my teachers were Norbertines.

I admired many of them and was impressed with

their friendships with each other. Most of them were young and content with their vocations.

I believe that this fact still exists today, even though we are much older and far smaller than those days. I like to think that the large numbers who have gone to God's house of infinite joy, especially Abbots Pennings, Killeen and Mackin, are interceding for us, pleading with Jesus and Mary for a healthy increase once again for our community. We have friends yet in "high places," and I invoke them when I can. We have new recruits who appear very promising. I think of Christ's parable of the mustard seed, the smallest possible, that one day grows into a bush large enough to house birds. That's our model and it will work.

Saints have been noted for their joy in the midst of pain and death. Such was the case of St. Thomas More at the moment of his execution. He was condemned to death by beheading on the false testimony of a witness at his trial. To the heads-man he says, "Friend, be not afraid of your office. You send me to God." More's nemesis, Cramner the chancellor replied, "You're very sure of that, Sir Thomas." More takes off his hat and joyfully replies, "He will not refuse one who is so blithe to go to him." (*A Man for All Seasons* by Robert Bolt.)

In one of the most beautiful scenes in the Bible, Jesus outlines the reward for those who feed the poor, clothe the naked, visit the sick and those in jail, give water to the thirsty and welcome the stranger. "Come you, who are blessed by my Father, inherit the kingdom prepared for you." (cf. Mt 25:31–45) In an earlier passage, Jesus uses the parable of the talents to address the issue of responsibility with the talents received and the outcome of joy. To the faithful servant who made five more talents from the five he received, the master cheerfully says, "Since you were faithful in small matters, I will give you great responsibilities. Come share your Master's joy." (Mt 25:23)

Candidates will be able to see one or another of us caring for the homeless, working with poor immigrants, visiting the sick, doctoring the indigenous natives in Peru, involved in conserving Catholic education at all levels, visiting prisoners each week, providing funds for Catholic ministries throughout our country, and a number of quiet and unseen missions that enrich our neighborhoods. I know we prefer to do this without bragging and that should be. I believe that we have the energy to fulfill Christ's parables of the talents and the challenge of the judgment outlined in Matthew 25:14–30 and 31–45.

On the west bank of the Fox River, St. Joseph Priory hosts a Norbertine community. It has done so from the time Father Bernard Pennings planted a community there in 1898. Laughter has echoed through its open windows in the spring and joy prevails when the snow piles up against its walls. We have inherited a precious secret: live with others in harmony. Pennings' motto on his coat of arms said it best: "Let us love each other."

Thank you for sharing my faith journey by reading this book. Pray for me.

Saint Benedict Press publishes books, Bibles, and multimedia that explore and defend the Catholic intellectual tradition. Our mission is to present the truths of the Catholic faith in an attractive and accessible manner.

Founded in 2006, our name pays homage to the guiding influence of the Rule of Saint Benedict and the Benedictine monks of Belmont Abbey, just a short distance from our headquarters in Charlotte, NC.

Saint Benedict Press publishes under several imprints. Our TAN Books imprint (TANBooks.com), publishes over 500 titles in theology, spirituality, devotions, Church doctrine, history, and the Lives of the Saints. Our Catholic Courses imprint (CatholicCourses.com) publishes audio and video lectures from the world's best professors in Theology, Philosophy, Scripture, Literature and more.

For a free catalog, visit us online at
SaintBenedictPress.com

Or call us toll-free at
(800) 437-5876

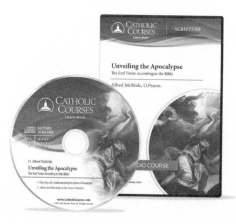

CATHOLIC COURSES

Learn More

A Tour of St. Peter's ▶ Square and Basilica

Exploring the History and Beauty of the Heart of Rome

Rev. Fr. Jeffrey Kirby, S.T.L.

In this course, Father Kirby takes a look at the history and artwork of St. Peter's square and basilica through the light of faith. This comprehensive tour explains why St. Peter's basilica was significant to the early Christians, and why it is still significant today. *Eight 30 minute lectures.*

978-1-61890-590-1 DVD / CD

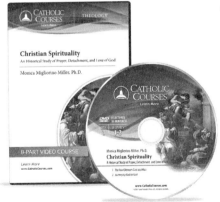

◀ The Spiritual Life

The Keys to Growing Closer to God

Rev. Fr. Jeffrey Kirby, S.T.L.

What does it mean to be close to God? In this course, Fr. Jeffrey Kirby will guide you through the most basic principles of the Spiritual Life, defining key terms and analyzing specific biblical verses that will greatly aid both newcomers to Christianity and those who have been Christians for years. *Eight 30 minute lectures.*

978-1-61890-612-0 DVD / CD

CatholicCourses.com • (800) 437-5876

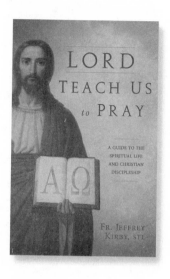